THE BUILDING DETECTIVE

A Journey Into the Hidden Stories of Property, People, and Problem Solving

Craig JL MacDonald

Copyright © Craig JL MacDonald 2025. All rights reserved.

First independently published 1 April 2025 in Australia via Kindle Direct Publishing.
Craig JL MacDonald asserts his right to be identified as the author of this work.

No part of this publication may be reproduced, distributed, or transmitted in any form or by any means, including photocopying, recording, or other electronic or mechanical methods, without the prior written permission of the author, except for brief quotations used in critical reviews or other non-commercial purposes permitted by copyright law.

The content of this book is provided for informational and entertainment purposes only and should not be relied upon as professional advice. While every effort has been made to ensure the accuracy of the information, the author and publisher make no representations or warranties regarding its completeness, accuracy, or applicability to your circumstances. Readers are advised to seek the assistance of a competent, appropriately qualified, and insured professional for advice specific to their situation. The author and publisher accept no responsibility for any loss, damage, or injury resulting from reliance on the information contained in this book.

This book is licensed for your personal use only. If you obtained this book without permission, please support the author by purchasing a legal copy.

Cover art and *The Building Detective* jigsaw branding were conceptualised by Frederick Alex Wales.

For permissions or inquiries, contact the author:
Email: info@thebuildingdetective.com
Mailing Address: PO Box 3103, Birkdale QLD 4159, Australia

ISBN:
Spot-gloss paperback:	978-1-7638952-0-1
KDP paperback:	978-1-7638952-1-8
eBook:	978-1-7638952-2-5
EPUB	978-1-7638952-3-2
Ingram paperback:	978-1-7638952-4-9

For Sarah,

Quinn & Jude

INTRODUCTION	1
PART I: BRING IN THE PROFESSIONAL	5
Chapter 1: The Intrepid Consultant	7
Chapter 2: The Legendary Detective	15
Chapter 3: The Master Storyteller	25
PART II: MAKING A CASE	33
Chapter 4: Concrete	35
Chapter 5: Masonry	45
Chapter 6: Timber	57
Chapter 7: Movement	71
Chapter 8: Water	85
Chapter 9: Deleterious Materials	111
PART III: CONTINUAL PROFESSIONAL DEVELOPMENT	137
Chapter 10: Building Services, Code Compliance & Contaminated Land	139
Chapter 11: Environment, Social & Governance	157
Chapter 12: Resilience	171
Chapter 13: Data & AI	187
EPILOGUE	211

ACKNOWLEDGMENTS	215
BIBLIOGRAPHY	221
FURTHER READING	235
INDEX OF BUILDINGS	239
LIST OF ABBREVIATIONS	241

Introduction

For the young, the need is to gain experience; for the experienced the need is to regain the enthusiasm of an open and questioning mind.

Malcolm Hollis, Surveying Buildings

Buildings are everywhere. We live in them, work in them, shop in them, and walk past them without a second thought. But beneath their surfaces, behind walls, beneath floors, and inside ceilings, buildings carry stories, mysteries, and lessons. Some are tales of brilliance and innovation, while others are cautionary reminders of what happens when things go wrong.

When I began my career as a Chartered Building Surveyor, I didn't expect to be piecing together puzzles like a detective. I thought I'd spend my days inspecting properties, ticking off compliance boxes, and writing reports. What I discovered was something far more compelling: every building holds a narrative, a blend of engineering, architecture, history, and human decisions that shape how it performs, fails, or thrives.

This book is not a textbook. It's a journey. Part memoir, part exploration of the property industry, and part practical guide to understanding the built environment. Although this book finds it home in Australia, and that is its primary context, it contains stories about buildings from around the world. Through the lens of my own experiences, I'll take you behind the scenes of real-world investigations and industry dilemmas, uncovering hidden defects while weaving in the human stories that underpin every structure.

You'll discover how ODEC, a codified approach to the scientific method, helps solve not just building problems but any problem. From high-profile building failures of the 2010s to tales from remote inspections in the Australian outback, you'll see how the decisions we make about our buildings affect not only their performance but also the people who live and work within them.

This book doesn't aim to catalogue every possible building problem (there are detailed textbooks for that). Instead, it's about curiosity. It's an invitation to look beyond surfaces and think critically about the spaces we inhabit and their context for generations to come. Whether you're a property professional, a homeowner, or simply someone who's ever wondered why water is coming into your home when it shouldn't, I hope you'll find insights, a new way of seeing the built world, and a renewed appreciation for inquisitiveness.

PART I: Bring In the Professional

Chapter 1: The Intrepid Consultant

My advice has no basis more reliable than my own meandering experience, be careful whose advice you buy but be patient with those who supply it.

Mary Schmich, whose essay became famous through Baz Luhrmann's spoken word song *Everybody's Free (To Wear Sunscreen)*[1]

More than 500 kilometres down a corrugated dirt track, with nothing but red dirt and spinifex in every direction, stood a school.

As far as the state government department responsible for the school was concerned, this school was a mystery. As in, it had no record of exactly what was there. Its best guess to date based only on the limited descriptions provided by its school principal whenever a problem needed to be addressed.

How could anyone make any decisions when the thing they're making decisions about was a mystery? Unidentified and unquantified?

Of over 800 schools in Western Australia, 37 of them are located in remote communities.[2] The sophistication of the Department's real estate team, the team responsible for budgeting for the repair, maintenance, and lifecycle replacement of its property portfolio, had graduated to requiring complete visibility of the physical condition of its portfolio. Including the hard-to-reach properties people rarely travelled to and from, let alone anyone from the Department.

The Building Detective

If this school was a 100-piece jigsaw puzzle, the Department was missing most of the pieces. They didn't even have the picture on the box. They had the four corners and most of the edges; they knew its location and how many children attended. Low resolution, out of date, aerial images showed blurred outlines of structures, at best. Ultimately, there was still no telling what the full picture was without sending someone who knew how to collect the rest of the pieces of the puzzle. It was the only way to fulfill the Department's mandate: the right to education for every child. Such a complex mandate includes providing fit for purpose environments.

Still, even the edges of the puzzle provided clues as to the full picture. It was enough information to plan an inspection based on estimating its size. Together with the same limited information provided for ten more remote schools, I had enough to propose a travel itinerary and devise a risk assessment. I was about to drive over 2,000 kilometres in nine days across Western Australia's outback, alone.

And I wasn't the only one. I was one of a team of consultants providing inspection and reporting coverage of the majority of the schools in the state. It was a very big puzzle with a lot of missing pieces, and we had the skills to know what each piece of this puzzle looked like, where and how to look for them. The Department, like the rest of our clients, paid us for the subjective interpretation of risk. To impart knowledge and advice which provide context, cost data, and a liability recourse. That is what nearly any type of consultant does. With this, the picture that should be on the front of the missing puzzle box, even with some pieces still missing, would reveal enough of itself. Finally, the Department would have enough confidence to make plans and decisions.

Consultant is a broad term; they exist in various fields, but consultants share something in common; they are problem solvers. What kind of consultant am I? I'm a building surveyor; armed with a knowledge of how buildings are built, a building surveyor's core skills include inspection and reporting methodology. If I wanted to

Chapter 1: The Intrepid Consultant

get real fancy, I could call myself a building pathologist; just as a doctor understands the human body so that they can diagnose problems, a building pathologist is able to do the same thing for buildings. The definition of building surveyor is slightly different in Australia from the rest of the world, so living and working here I'm referred to as a building consultant. Used by itself, the word "surveyor" is closely associated with the enormous national mining and engineering industries in Australia, and the work undertaken for them by cadastral surveyors. All types of surveyors, too, share something in common; they collect data.

****

I became a consultant by accident.

The first time anything to do with the built environment came onto my radar, and I don't mean playing with *LEGO* or *Meccano*, but as a way to make a living, was when I completed an aptitude test at school. An aptitude test is designed to assess what a person is capable of doing or to predict what a person is able to learn or do given the right education and instruction. It represents a person's level of competency to perform a certain type of task. The test produces about twenty results, in order of what the person may be most capable of doing. High school students are able to use the results from their test as a tool with their guidance counsellor to assist in choosing subjects for further study after the age of sixteen. For some reason, my top result was naval architecture.

This was odd. Even though I'm recalling this from over 25 years ago, I'm sure none of the questions were about boats. I had never indicated any interest in boats. Architecture, however, intrigued me. It came across as more realistic than being a palaeontologist at least, which had been my go-to job preference since seeing Jurassic Park at the age of ten.

I loved technical drawing. When I was in high school in Scotland in the nineties, the class that taught this was called Graphic

Communication. There were annual awards for best student in each subject, and whilst I was not stellar in all subjects, I was recognised with the award for best in school at Graphic Communication. The subject centred around learning how to draw technical drawings using a drawing board, T-square, and set squares. Today this work is completed using software called CAD (computer aided design). Technical drawing was one of those tasks where I found flow: a state in which you are so involved in an activity that nothing else seems to matter.

As it turned out, architecture degrees favoured a high grade in Graphic Communication. However, they favoured something else even more: high grades in maths and physics. I was okay in maths, but not A-grade material, and I found physics difficult to grasp. My school guidance counsellor knew this too, and candidly admitted "I don't think you're going to get the grades you need to get accepted into an architecture degree. Is there anything else you like?"

Around that time, my Dad and I had built a computer together. It was pretty straightforward. You buy around seven key components: a motherboard, a CPU, a heat sink fan, a hard drive, a power supply unit, and back then you'd buy a floppy disc drive and maybe a CD-ROM drive too. Attach them all together inside a case and you've "built" a computer. Plug in your keyboard, mouse and monitor, install an operating system on it, and away you go. I was obsessed. It was around the time home internet access was really taking off. A month wouldn't go by without an AOL free trial CD being popped through your letterbox. Friends and I figured out how to chat to each other, among other things, using the internet. I was soon teaching myself how to animate using Macromedia Flash, software for animating images along paths of motion, instead of frame-by-frame movement.

"I like computers, and I want to be an animator." Animating an idea on my computer was another one of those things that gave me deep flow.

Chapter 1: The Intrepid Consultant

"Maybe you should consider dropping Advanced Higher Graphic Communication, and take Higher Computing instead?" (Higher and Advanced Higher qualifications were Scotland's equivalent to entry level grades required for entry into higher education)

Imparting advice specific to their area of expertise is the primary thing a consultant does. The "advice" can take many forms: a report, a strategy, a workshop, an investigation, and so on. The funny thing about advice is its complexion changes depending on whether you've asked for it, and if you've asked for it, maybe you're even paying to get it. If it's offered up to you without you asking for it, anything you do with that advice is entirely at your own risk.

I took my guidance counsellor's advice. I did not elect Advance Higher Graphic Communication. Instead, I elected Higher Computing, which I eventually failed anyway. My grades however, on the whole, were enough to land me a conditional offer to study Bachelor of Science in Computer Science with an honours year in multimedia studies at Heriot-Watt University in Edinburgh. No one forced me to take that advice, the choice was mine, based on the information I had available to me. I hadn't realised it, but I had experienced one of the first things about how a consultant discharges their role for their clients: they furnish them with information, communicated in plain language, which contributes to making decisions. Perhaps if I had spent more energy collecting more information, I might have made a different, more informed decision.

The first year of Computer Science was nearing its end. I was learning, with mixed results, how to code using Java. After the novelty wore off, I didn't find it fun and there was a lot of sitting down. It was beginning to dawn on me that this might not be something I want to make a living from. At the start of the final term before the summer holidays, I was half asleep in a lecture theatre, when the lecturer said something that woke me right up, "...and next year you'll be doing C++." The lecture had barely begun, and I left. Without an appointment, I beelined to my tutor's office, realising that I did not want to spend a career solely in front of a computer.

"I want to change courses. I don't want to do Computer Science anymore".

"I see. What would you like to change to?" clearly, he was used to this. I lived in a hall of residence and had made friends whose subjects were located in the university's School of the Built Environment. I was burning to correct a decision I regretted, "Any subject in the School of the Built Environment." He handed me the prospectus. As we chatted, I ran my finger down bullet point lists for subjects I'd never heard of. One of them was Building Surveying and one of its bullet points read technical drawing.

"I want to change to Building Surveying". Of course, it wasn't as simple as that, but after ironing out the details I was accepted into BSc (Hons) Building Surveying, albeit right back to the start of year one. Noting I moved to Australia with my qualification and eventually became a citizen, the term 'building surveyor' has a slightly different understanding in Australia than it does for the rest of the world. Outside of Australia 'building surveyor' reflects the definition provided by the Royal Institution of Chartered Surveyors (RICS), as someone with a broad skillset whose core competencies include identifying building defects. This is the definition adopted by this book. The definition of a building surveyor provided by the Australian Institute of Building Surveyors (AIBS) is someone who is an expert in volumes one and two of Australia's National Construction Code (NCC): the Building Code of Australia. Their focus is solely on building code compliance (which I explore a little more in Chapter 10).

It was nearly three more years, including repeating a year because of low grades, before I found myself in a real-life consultant's office. Although my degree covered all manner of technical subjects specific to a building surveyor (history of the built environment, construction technology, principles of structures, engineering

Chapter 1: The Intrepid Consultant

materials, site investigation and surveying, etc.) there was very little focus on what it means to be a professional or a consultant. The true way to learn about this was via work experience, but I didn't know that yet. My default thinking was to get a degree and to get a job, in that order. One day my Dad blurts out, "oh, I think I know a building surveyor. Maybe you could get some work experience from him?"

My Dad had known a partner at Hardies Property Consultants via a networking event they attended together for years, called "the Breakfast Club". Why it took four years for it to occur to him that information would have meant something to me sooner, remains with his ashes. Still, it led to a casual meet up and a *Sliding Doors* moment. A meeting was arranged. The partner, Craig Gilmour, was agreeable, "Absolutely. You can come as little or as often as you like. We can't pay you right away, but as long as you're studying, you're welcome to shadow our surveyors."

On days without lectures, I shadowed Hardies' building surveyors (and on nights I worked in an Edinburgh pub kitchen). It was winter in Scotland, the ground was frozen solid, and I was in someone's back yard holding a clip board and jotting measurements someone was shouting to me from a dumpy level. After that I was in the roof space of a hundreds-year-old stone cottage, using a laser measure to record dimensions of the space, and taking as many photographs as possible. I was going to draw the site up in CAD when we got back to the office. My fingertips were freezing, my feet were wet, and I forgot to bring any snacks. But I wasn't stuck at a desk and here I was mucking around in some village miles from the office. It was a bit of an adventure. That was the first time I thought, "Yeah, I could do this as a job."

For the next year and a half, I got to travel around central east Scotland as a student building surveyor. Exploring new places quickly became my favourite part of the job. It didn't matter where I travelled to, if it was a new place, it was always adventurous. You get to travel to somewhere you'd never been before and speak to new people all the time. At this very beginning point of my consulting career however, I was not consulting. I spent much of my time observing how my colleagues worked, noting how they approached client needs and translated those into actionable scopes of work. All the while, their spoken and written communication was on full display. I'd provide support in the delivery of the scope of work, which was generally the execution part. More often than not, I was collecting data. This took many forms, such as measurements that would help prepare drawings, or descriptions of the condition of various building elements along with any noteworthy observations. Photographs would support nearly anything, as a means of conferring with colleagues or documenting supporting evidence for a recommendation or a conclusion. Whether it was determining their repair obligations at the end of a lease, advising on how to install a fire hydrant riser to meet code, identifying how to build a kitchen extension, or solving the mystery of a mouldy damp patch below Mrs. MacAllister's bay window, we had to gather as much information as we could to enable us to provide the clearest possible advice on which decisions could call themselves informed.

Chapter 2: The Legendary Detective

Maddy:

Jonathan, we're looking at a scenario for which there is absolutely no conceivable explanation.

Jonathan:

There's always an explanation. You've just got to think round corners. Don't always see what you're meant to see.

Jonathan Creek[1]

You don't have to be a building surveyor to call yourself someone who collects data and solves problems. All of us do both every day. You do it when your train is delayed, or when you run out of milk at 6am. You've done it to complete a jigsaw puzzle.

Let's say you've got yourself a thousand-piece puzzle. What are some of the first things you do? You begin to problem solve. First you break down the task. You begin with searching for the edge pieces, each straight edge jumping out from the pile. If you're lucky, you come across all four corners during this first step. The pieces with edges, together with the corners, are all data points. It's information you already know how to identify, structure, and how they relate to each other. Once you've identified the edges, you've defined the scope of your problem.

Once a lot of edges have been collected, it starts getting harder and there's not as many edges jumping out of the pile any more.

The Building Detective

However, as you collected edges, you may have noticed something else. Colour groups begin to emerge from the image on the box. This discovery naturally leads to the next step: sorting similar coloured pieces into their own piles.

You've broken the problem of solving the jigsaw puzzle into distinct tasks which you can now close out one by one until the puzzle is solved. As you progress, a picture becomes clearer and clearer. The puzzle is not yet complete, but you're now able to confirm with a high degree of confidence that it is indeed the picture that is on the box and can describe it adequately to someone else. This jigsaw metaphor is a simple way to describe how detectives work, indeed how building consultants work, or how anyone solves a mystery.

The strange thing about being a professional building pathologist, is that I've never constructed anything with my bare hands. All of my knowledge, especially in the beginning, was read. Such is university; a particular challenge for someone who learns by doing and learns even more by failing. To find yourself assessing the condition of the built form, having only ever seen its concealed elements, its substrate, in diagrams within textbooks, is enough to make you feel out of your depth. A lot of imagination and visualisation is put to work and continually exercised when learning construction technology; the subject of understanding construction materials, techniques and processes. Today, resources like YouTube offer invaluable insights, allowing you to see construction processes in action. You can freely watch detailed animations of how materials come together, in what order, and how elements should interface. For someone learning to visualise what's hidden beneath a building's finishes, this kind of resource bridges the gap between theoretical knowledge and practical understanding ...without ever visiting a construction site.

Sight isn't the only sense at our disposal. Observations are the sum of all our senses working together to perceive the world around us. Smell picks up the musty notes of dampness or fungus, springing a

Chapter 2: The Legendary Detective

new line of inquiry. Hearing is engaged when tapping plasterboard or ceramic tiles reveals a hollow sound, indicating a void where there shouldn't be one. Touch, such as feeling heat radiating from an internal wall, may suggest that insulation has deteriorated or dropped, no longer shielding the room from the sun-blasted brick veneer wall on the other side. Each sense contributes a piece of the puzzle.

Building detectives don't stop at their senses alone. An arsenal of devices and equipment are at their disposal that either collect data or augment their senses. As clues and questions continue to reveal new lines of inquiry, equipment helps progress each inquiry as much as possible, hopefully to the point where the line of inquiry can be eliminated. Elimination should provide a sense of satisfaction as it is genuine progress. Once we've tested all of our hypotheses, deductions, theories and correlations, then done all we can to disprove what remains, we may have arrived at our best guess as to the cause, or collection of causes of an issue. A *possible* conclusion.

Solving a problem can be approached in two ways: deductively or comparatively. Deduction involves drawing connections between observations and testing ideas to see if they fit the evidence. The comparative process, on the other hand, matches the evidence to known characteristics of potential causes. There is always a danger in deciding as to the cause of a problem too quickly, particularly if for each problem there may be many causes that could fit the observations or data. Conclusions must arise from critical thought and not just the first thing that comes to mind. The feeling of triumph that comes with being right can be a very strong one. When we have this feeling, it's wise to practice recognising it and being real with yourself. Ask yourself what's more important; being right or the truth? Prioritising the truth not only ensures accurate conclusions but also fosters trust with clients who value honesty and transparency over a false sense of certainty. The answer is clear to a professional acting with integrity: they acknowledge when they lack sufficient information and are transparent about their limitations.

Broadly speaking, the whole process reflects the scientific method, the process of objectively establishing facts through testing and experimentation: observations, deduction, elimination, and finally a conclusion. I offer **ODEC**.

Observations

This means in the broadest possible terms, all of the relevant data you can get your hot hands on. It includes all your observations, be it visual, or collected using equipment. It includes documentation and interviews. An observation that's often neglected at first, but can be critical, relates to the dimension of time. It's easy to see how this can be neglected, we are all pressed for time, held to deadlines for deliverables. We often don't have the luxury of observing if something changes or presents new information when viewed across four seasons. However, the detective will do themselves a disservice if they do not consider perspective. Perspective represents multiple opportunities to collect relevant new observations. Bringing your eyes to the ground and looking upwards or reviewing something in the context of years instead of hours. Make sure you spend time looking for longer-term, slower-paced information. If you're standing two metres in front of a wall, make sure to walk back and look at the wall in its widest possible context. Multiple perspectives are the key.

There are pitfalls in collecting observations. In his great book, *The Data Detective*, Tim Harford shows us that we shouldn't immediately trust data simply based on the reputation of its source, or the way it's presented.

29

The number of words in the preceding sentence.[2]

Never dismiss the possibility for an agenda to manipulate data, or for research to produce data that is simply erroneous. The correct number is actually 32. The observation stage of our investigation

Chapter 2: The Legendary Detective

permits us to collect such data, as we'll take responsibility for testing it and thereby possibly eliminating it. 'Trust, but verify' serves as a reminder that the scientific method demands thorough scrutiny; every observation, no matter the source, must be tested and validated before it can be relied upon.[3]

At this stage we'll collect everything we can that might be relevant to our investigation. Including asking questions and simply listening and recording. Good questions are those crafted in such a way that they can draw out new evidence. As demonstrated by our dummy statistic, facts can be misleading, whereas rumours, true or false, can be revealing.[4] We revealed a truth that something can be wrong, or the possibility that something is being hidden. Like Edison noted of his experiments, "I've not failed, I've found 10,000 ways that don't work."

Deductions, Correlations, Theories & Hypotheses

We want to reach a conclusion, and producing deductions is one way to get there. We deduce when we propose a conclusion by applying logical rules to premises. This allows us to reach a conclusion that must be true if the premises are true. It's time to use all of our observations to get down to business.

I've included other language that features in the scientific method. For simplicity, I've grouped them under *deduction*s in ODEC, even though some, like correlations and hypotheses, arise more from inductive reasoning. Lumping them under D for *deduction* creates a memorable mnemonic device that is also phonic: *OH-deck* (/ˈoʊ.dɛk/). The other linked activities I've grouped with *deduction* are identifying correlations, developing theories, and forming hypotheses.

A correlation is a mutual relationship between two things. For example, if ice cream sales rise at the same time as sunburn cases, the two are correlated, but one doesn't cause the other. Both are actually influenced by a third factor: hot weather. So, correlation does not imply causation. Causation means one thing causes another, in other words, action A *causes* outcome B. Correlations are symmetrical. Proving that they are correlated is proving nothing more than their data is linearly symmetrical. Identifying a correlation means you still have to prove causation.

A theory is a well-supported explanation for something, built from observations and hypotheses. Which brings us neatly to the last *Inception*-level of DCTH: the hypothesis; a testable statement about the relationship between two or more variables, or a proposed explanation for an observation. Of each of the logic statements that are created from this process, you should be able to rephrase them as sharp, well-defined questions. The discipline of refining big, nebulous ideas into crisp, testable hypotheses is what separates good science from unthoughtful speculation.

Sometimes, solving problems requires stepping outside your usual way of thinking. Our habits and perspectives often shape how we approach challenges, which can limit the solutions we see. Consider the tomato sauce example. Take two types of people: one keeps the tomato sauce in the cupboard and the other person keeps their tomato sauce in the fridge. When the person who keeps the sauce in the cupboard runs out of sauce, they look for alternatives in the cupboard, perhaps finding things like mustards or BBQ sauce. Where does the other person look when they run out of tomato sauce? They look in the fridge and their alternatives are altogether different; mayonnaise and so forth. Sometimes you have to acknowledge that your brain thinks a certain way, to be able to release yourself to be open to an altogether different way of thinking. Consider the following sentence for example: Thiss sentence has threee errors. At first glance, you might miss one, or even all of them. This highlights how easy it is to overlook details when you're not deliberately observing. Whether it's a typo or a structural defect, taking the time to look closely can reveal much more than you initially notice.[5]

Chapter 2: The Legendary Detective

In her book *A Mind for Numbers* Barbara Oakley explains how our brain works when it is solving a problem. She proposes it has two modes: focus and diffuse mode. Focus mode is self-explanatory. Diffuse mode is when your brain works on a problem in the background while you focus on something else. It's why great ideas often come during a run, a drive, or even in the shower. That's when you're not actively trying to solve the problem. When we take a break from working on a problem our brain continues to tinker away with it in the background, especially when you've managed to turn your attention to something else. Even when you're asleep. I often have these ah-ha moments when I go for a run or when I'm driving (when I'm unable to easily create notes!) You might have heard the saying; anyone who's had a shower has had an idea. Though a different, rarer type of person will follow up with the execution.

Elimination

You now inch closer to the finish line by regarding your list of DCTH and starting with just one, figure out how to rule it out. Prove it wrong. Test it. Elimination may draw out further questions and produce more deductions. This loop will get smaller as you begin to rule each DCTH out. When you are left with just one, it *might* be the conclusion. When you are left with more than one, consider that they might all be true. In building pathology, multiple causes often interrelate to create a single issue. For example, a leaking roof might result not just from a deteriorated membrane but also from blocked gutters, poor design, and insufficient maintenance. Each factor contributes to the problem, and addressing only one may not fully resolve it. Recognising this complexity ensures a more holistic and effective solution.

Conclusion

For a building pathologist, reaching a conclusion, or a probable conclusion, is the same as reaching a diagnosis; determining the nature and cause of an issue. A conclusion is often coveted as a kind of perfect, infallible explanation for your problem or issue. Often however, this is unrealistic and for complex issues, not possible. An incomplete puzzle can still reveal the full picture; likewise, a collection of probable conclusions can guide action. It's a mark of a careful professional to ensure this point is made clear. A good level of probability should still be enough comfort to be able to reasonably act upon and make decisions.

Now we can move onto everyone's favourite part of solving a mystery: the part where the enigmatic detective stands before the interested parties to deliver the dramatic reveal. They don't simply show their cards, no. They tell a story.

Chapter 3: The Master Storyteller

Never let the truth get in the way of a good story.

Mark Twain

Stories have the power to connect us through time. Humans have been doing this for a very long time. In his book *The Hero With a Thousand Faces*, the late professor of literature, Joseph Campbell, describes the 'monomyth'.[1] A framework for "the hero's journey" and how he observed this framework in action. Whether in cave paintings, Greek mythology, or religious texts, this framework appears repeatedly. Today, the framework is used to create effective advertising and marketing campaigns as well as commercially viable multi-million-dollar movies. There may only be one story being retold over and over again, being changed slightly each time. We are always drawn in. In matters of love, family, life, and death, we are drawn in over and over again. This framework is not limited to that of the trials of a journeying hero. A consultant can also use it to effectively communicate their findings to their client (perhaps take Mark Twain's suggestion with a pinch of salt, however). The point isn't to embellish the truth but to recognise the power of storytelling as a tool to communicate meaning. So powerful that we don't care when it's fictional if it reveals some truth or meaning to us. Use it wisely.

Campbell's framework proposes that everyone is the hero of their own story. When you start to look out at life and those around you through this lens, you are not at the centre. Suddenly you aren't the only person with problems. And just like that you're empathising. You're connecting yourself to other people by putting yourself in their shoes. Just as you are the hero of your story, complete strangers who will never meet or see again are each the hero of their own story. In this way, you can empathise with your client as you walk them through the journey of the problem, they need your help to solve, or even use the framework as a guide to see where you currently are on the journey of any given problem.

So we can understand how to apply this framework to telling the story of a mystery, let's first take a look at the monomyth; the standard path identified by Campbell:

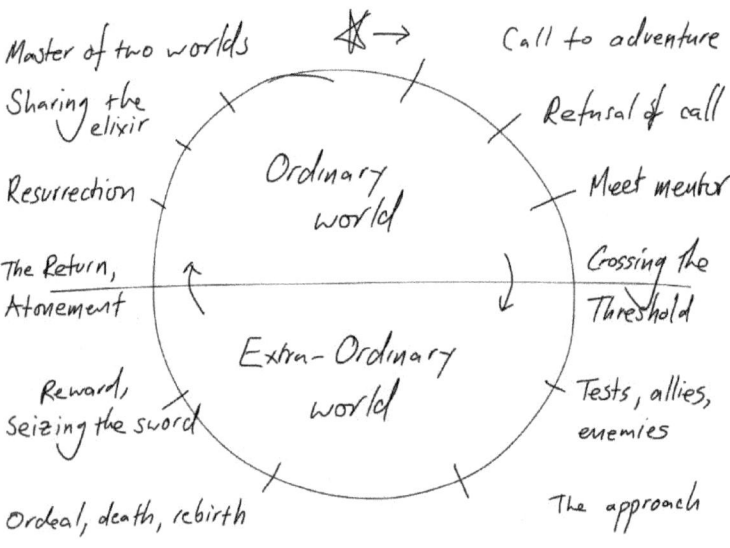

Chapter 3: The Master Storyteller

In *The Writer's Journey*, Chris Vogler shows how he applied Campbell's work in his role as story fixer at Disney over a period of 20 years. Campbell's work inspired George Lucas to write and make Star Wars.[2] Movies, especially children's movies, are structured and produced using this framework as part of maximising commercial success. Once you recognise the various structural elements to the framework, they're quite easy to spot. The framework is an effective tool with broad application. Here's what your or your client's journey might look like through this lens:

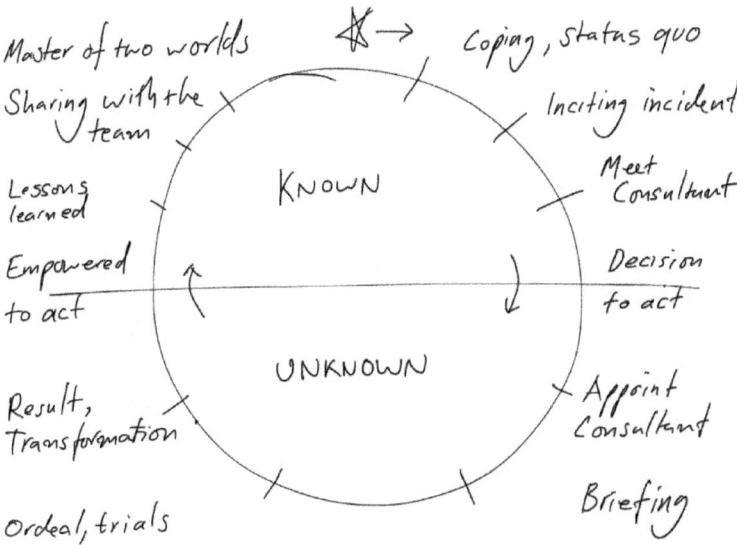

Nathan is an accountant who sits on a body corporate committee that manages an apartment complex. In Australia, a body corporate is the legal entity that manages the common property of residential, commercial, retail, industrial or mixed-used properties. They are also referred to as Community Title Strata, or CTS. Variations of this exist in other countries, as we'll see in this book's case studies, such as tenant management organisations in the UK, condo associations, or homeowner associations in the USA. Common property can include shared assets like car parks, grounds and lifts.

The Building Detective

He doesn't realise it yet, but Nathan is about to embark on a journey.

- In Nathan's ordinary world, life is business as usual and problems are predictable. Nathan is an accountant, and outside of his accounting day job, he sits on a committee that is responsible for the running and upkeep of common areas in an apartment block where he owns one of the apartments. Nathan's knowledge of buildings stops about there.

- Something disrupts business as usual. Whatever coping mechanisms that may have been in place up to that point no longer work. There is cracked concrete in the car park basement of the 10-storey apartment complex and no one on the committee really knows what this means for the building. The committee is made up of various apartment owners, a diverse mix of backgrounds and professions, but no one works in property or construction.

- Fearing the worst, that the apartment block needs to be demolished, someone on the committee who works in finance concludes they need to first estimate the property's economic life; that is to ask, what is the cost of the minimum repairs or replacements required to the property, for it to continue to perform as required (as a safe dwelling for multiple residential occupants; and as a stable return on investment for owners), before it is estimated to be more cost effective to demolish and redevelop the site. Nathan is friends with someone who works in a property company in the city and offers to make an enquiry as to who can assist. The committee has made the decision to act. Nathan crosses the threshold into the unknown.

- Nathan makes his phone call to his property friend, asking "is there such a thing as a consultant ...for buildings?" His friend is sure there is and knows someone that can help and passes Nathan the details of a building consultant.

- Nathan describes his journey so far to the consultant, he's not really been exposed to this stuff before and is hoping that the

Chapter 3: The Master Storyteller

consultant can guide him. He has finally met the mentor of his quest. A mentor in the hero's journey is an ex-hero himself and has tread this path before. He typically gifts the hero with something he can use on his quest. The building consultant reverse briefs Nathan's rough requirements, outlining the next steps on his journey.

- Journeying deeper into the extraordinary world of building consultancy, Nathan appoints the building consultant to undertake a full building inspection and to prepare a sinking fund forecast report; a report that predicts the replacement and repair costs to the common property of a strata titled building like Nathan's apartment block. Upon receipt of the report, Nathan's fears were transformed into confidence and hope.

- With the report in hand, Nathan journeys back into the known, ordinary, world and tables it at the next body corporate meeting, sharing with the committee the lessons he has learned from his journey into the unknown. The committee now understand, not only that the nature of the cracking is not cause for alarm but is also empowered with an accurate forecast on how to maintain the whole building for the next ten years, ensuring the apartment owners' annual body corporate fees are being spent wisely and that everyone's investment is being protected.

Context is paramount. All of the observations you collate contribute to your context. It will always be possible that you're missing a critical observation, an important piece of information, something that has the potential to influence context. Context is the circumstances that form the setting and shared understanding of more than one person. For example, Stonehenge is considered to be in a fair condition based on its age, use and location. This is fine because it is likely that between you and I, we already have a shared understanding of Stonehenge's context. In most cases, for the buildings we report on, we have to build that context up first to ensure that there is no ambiguity that a shared understanding has formed. We do this using simple, clear language, avoiding platitudes or vague expressions such as "it was REALLY massive", or "it was quite small". These are subjective to individual interpretation and provide no benchmark for another's understanding. Be mindful when using probabilistic language, as it can be interpreted in different ways. For example: "it's possible"; "unlikely"; and "almost certain". Any report providing advice and recommendations should include clear definitions of these terms to create a baseline for understanding between the author and the reader. Using ambiguous, subjective, or exaggerated language introduces significant professional risks. If your report is open to varying interpretations, miscommunication can lead to disputes, misunderstandings, or even legal action. Using clear, precise language ensures your findings are understood as intended, protecting both you and your client from unnecessary complications.

Your story will require the explicit statement of exclusions, inclusions, limitations and caveats as part of removing as much ambiguity as possible. This story is not a creative work of fiction and should not be open to interpretation. For it is such ambiguity that can lead to one's interpretation being decided upon in court. Interpretation becomes an even greater risk when you attempt to tell your story using data. In order to do this effectively, you have to first interpret what the data is telling you. This alone is fraught with risk, especially if you are operating in a silo. It's common for you to gravitate toward anything that matches your gut feel or first guess. Confirmation bias is a tendency to evaluate evidence and test arguments in a way that's biased toward our own preconceptions. Telling a story using data is powerful because information can be illustrated in such a way to convey complex information quickly and to a broad range of learning styles and readers. However, telling a story in this way is a skill in itself. Tread carefully and if you must, seek appropriate expertise.

Malcolm Hollis reminds us that our report must be based upon a reflection of the consequences of what has been observed. He said

Chapter 3: The Master Storyteller

this before the advent of mobile devices and it remains true: reporting should not be done on site, like the "do it once" form-filling apps of today, because you sacrifice an important part of the investigating and storytelling process: reflecting on your findings. Recall our mnemonic from the previous chapter, ODEC: Observations, Deduction, Elimination, and Conclusion. Advice in the form of a warning to its target reader must contain several elements: a simple statement, a warning, your opinion, then your advice.[3] This is where ODEC must be used carefully to illustrate the logical journey from context to advice, ensuring that any remaining gaps or questions are caveated. If you have moved through ODEC, then you will have all the pieces of the puzzle needed to apply to the Campbellian framework and effectively and clearly tell your story.

You're about to cross the threshold from Part 1 of this book, to embark on a journey exploring case studies which form the basis of Part 2. Consider ODEC the gift received from the mentor, a boon, from which you'll draw for support on your quest through the extraordinary world of being a Building Detective.

PART II: Making a Case

Chapter 4: Concrete

There is a crack in everything, that's how the light gets in

Leonard Cohen

On the morning of Christmas Eve 2018, residents of the brand new, 36-storey, Opal Tower in Sydney's Olympic Park suddenly heard unusual loud bangs apparently coming from the building itself. By the afternoon a resident on the tenth floor called Australia's emergency services, reporting a crack, presumably a visual description as well as an audible one. Police arrived to discover a crack to a precast concrete panel located at a balcony on level ten. To most people, a crack is a crack; to a building detective, it's a clue with a unique story to tell.

Most solid materials crack along their weakest route when pulled apart in tension; the state of being stretched tight. If something has good tensile strength, it will not easily yield when stretched. In the context of a building element being stretched tightly in two opposite directions, normally those directions are upwards and downwards. It's not often that movement is upwards (but possible). Downwards is the most common direction to create tension as buildings are heavy and subject to gravity like the rest of us.

The Building Detective

Since buildings are heavy, their weight has to travel somewhere. The weight produced by buildings is referred to as "load" and buildings are designed to make sure loads are directed appropriately to safely reach a suitable geological foundation, like rock. Directing loads in such a way ensures undue stress is not put on any single element, that everything is as strong as it needs to be to withstand certain loads. The Australian Standard for concrete structures, AS3600, outlines the loads that can be tolerated by certain concrete specifications.[1] Even loads imposed upon a structure from outside, like wind for example, eventually travel downward through a structure because of gravity. Since loads travel downward, load at the bottom of a wall is greater than the load at top of a wall. Naturally we want to construct using the minimum quantity of materials so we're not spending more money than we need to. So, we design to these standards, and if we didn't, we'd have all sorts of cracks all over the place, presenting risks all the way up to structural failure and building collapse.

One more characteristic of cracks worth explaining before we proceed is delamination, also known as spalling. Imagine a croissant. Layers of baked, buttery bread dough produced through a proving process called lamination. The dough is proved, then flattened and folded onto itself, and proved again. The process is repeated for a few days to create the beautiful, layered lamination we all recognise in croissants. The way the top crispy layer of your croissant comes away is delamination. It is the same characteristic we can observe to the face of concrete when it has a crack layer concealed underneath, eventually pushing the broken section of concrete off.

Cracks at Opal Tower didn't just slowly develop, creeping in length and width over a long period of time like most cracks do. Consistent with reports of loud bangs, these cracks were caught appearing on CCTV. What police were looking at was more than just a crack; it was roughly a half metre section of a face of a prefabricated concrete panel, at the bottom of a wall connecting to a concrete

Chapter 4: Concrete

beam at floor level. The face of the concrete wall panel was beginning to delaminate away from the wall. Understandably, for such a dramatic crack to suddenly appear in an instant would strike enough fear in you to at least call emergency services, if not immediately run out of the building. The police did the former and called the fire and rescue service. After inspecting the crack themselves, the fireys (as Australians affectionately call them) ordered the evacuation of around 3,000 residents from Opal Tower as well as nearby buildings. Furthermore, they created a 250m radius exclusion zone, disconnected gas and water, and isolated the tower from the electricity grid whilst engineers appointed by the state government attended to try to figure out what was going on. The engineers' scope of work was not only to assess the structural integrity to determine if residents could safely reoccupy their homes, but to investigate a number of matters relating to the cracking of the concrete and the likely causes of the cracking.

Just three weeks following the incident, the investigators issued their interim report. It featured a number of their initial hypotheses for the cause of the cracks:

- Environmental factors, such as wind or temperature changes;
- Use of poor-quality construction materials;
- Foundation issues;
- Inadequate structural design; and
- Poor workmanship during construction.

In their final report they show how they followed a process of testing each hypothesis in detail, eliminating those pieces of the jigsaw that clearly did not fit the edges and corners they already had. Whilst their interim report was able to conclude that the building was in an overall structurally sound condition and not in danger of collapse, their final report built upon their initial conclusions. The cracking was a result of inadequate structural design per Australia's National Construction Code (NCC),[2] and AS3600 for concrete structures. The under-designed concrete hob beams were susceptible to failure by shear compression. Shearing is similar to tension, where two forces are thrusting in opposite directions, but they are offset, compressing past each other.

A concrete hob beam is a beam which rests on the edge of a concrete slab to further strengthen it to receive point loads from the likes of concrete columns transferring loads from above. Imagine a point load like your weight pushing an umbrella into the ground, versus spreading the load out, like how skis spread out to stop you sinking into snow. The hob beam is like the ski and is the concrete element the cracked precast concrete wall panel was connected to. The engineers' tested their hypotheses by comparing the observed conditions on-site to the original design drawings and the requirements of the National Construction Code and Australian Standards. This comparative approach aligns with the ODEC framework by using evidence to match observations with potential causes, eliminating those that don't fit the puzzle, and narrowing in on the most likely explanation.

The investigation found a number of workmanship issues too, including inadequate grouting (the seal made between beams and panels), wrongly constructed widths of pre-cast panels and insufficient tensile capacity caused by the use of incorrectly sized reinforcing bars. The damage to the beam was made worse by the progressive increase of live loads as residents moved in. One might hypothesise that this was the straw that broke the camel's back. Live loads are distinguished from dead loads. Dead loads are what we discussed as being the heavy elements of the building's structure that typically don't change for its whole lifecycle. Live load is weight that moves around, comes and goes. Like people, cars, or snow. Design must consider the possible contributions of live loads too.

With the final report's conclusions, a builder could make informed decisions on the methodology for repair, also referred to as rectification. Planning and executing the repair project also provides an indicative timeframe for directly impacted residents to reoccupy

Chapter 4: Concrete

their homes, which the report advised that the building designers must ensure that no structural member is overloaded before residents move back in. The builder had to take responsibility for residents' temporary accommodation costs ($8.5 million AUD[3]), as well as the cost of rectifications ($17 million AUD). Residents began to move in nine months after the evacuation, even though some temporary props holding weight remained in place. It was 2022 before a class action lawsuit of Opal Tower unit owners seeking compensation from New South Wales (NSW) Government (the original developer for the Olympic Park site), reached an out of court settlement of $7.3 million AUD excluding legal costs. Something to consider in light of the compensation is the reputational impact that will forever remain with each property in the tower, expected to diminish each apartment's ability to rise in value or be easily resold, effectively destroying investments.

****

Concrete cancer is a commonly misused term, erroneously referring to carbonation. Concrete cancer is the nickname given to alkali-silica-reaction (ASR), which was first diagnosed in the United States in the 1940s. It has this nickname because there is 'no known cure' for ASR. ASR is caused when alkaline chemicals present in cement react with silica; the substance occurring naturally in certain types of aggregate or stone used to make concrete. The reaction produces a jelly like substance around the stones, which absorb water and expand. The expansion causes cracks in the concrete. If water gets in and freezes, the cracks become wider and let in still more water. The steel reinforcement is then vulnerable to water penetration and corrosion takes place causing further defects. The cracks develop slowly and become noticeable long before there is any major danger. The problem can be avoided in new building work using a low alkali cement or by avoiding the use of chemically reactive aggregates. ASR isn't a defect I've personally come across in my experience, however, it's common to older road infrastructure in the UK, such as concrete bridges and flyovers. The sheen of the aforementioned jelly like substance can be observed even when passing under by car.

Concrete is strong in compression, and as we've seen, this is a performance characteristic we need for heavy, tall buildings. Given it is a comparatively cheap material to produce and has an accepted useful life of at least 75 years, it is the most widely used construction material today. However, concrete is weak in tension. To mitigate this characteristic, the mix is poured around steel reinforcement bars, increasing the concrete's strength in tension. However, steel is susceptible to corrosion, which expands the steel and causes delamination. In materials science corrosion is a broad term describing deterioration of metals due to chemical reactions with their environment (and rust, the red-brown flaky coating, is a result of corrosion). Corrosion occurs when the reinforcement bars are exposed to oxygen; a chemical process called oxidation. Structurally sound concrete has a high pH ($\sim$12.0 – 13.3) making it an alkaline environment for the reinforcement bars. When the alkalinity of concrete is lost, this is known as carbonation. This can occur either due to a poor mix, environmental conditions or a combination of these variables adding to their age. It is this alkalinity that protects the steel reinforcement within the concrete from corrosion by causing a protective film to form around it, sealing the steel off from the effects of the environment, including oxygen. The protection is called "passivation" or referred to as a passive protective layer around the reinforcement. When carbonation occurs, the passive protective layer is gone, leaving the concrete's reinforcement bars susceptible to corrosion. Carbonation does not cause corrosion; it just creates the conditions for corrosion of the steel reinforcement bars to occur.

Phenolphthalein (pronounced fee-nol-thay-leen), a common diagnostic tool, is a widely available chemical compound sprayed onto concrete to indicate the alkalinity of its pH level. Where spray colour turns from clear to purple, there is a high alkalinity indicating no carbonation; otherwise healthy concrete. Although, one cannot simply spray the exposed surface of concrete and expect to learn much. Passivation is the precise reason that the steel reinforcement has a minimum required depth or coverage from the surface. Think of the surface and its first 20-30 millimetres of depth being allowed to lose its alkalinity, a sort of sacrificial depth, with the reinforcement remaining far enough away from the environmental factors that can compromise it. Not achieving the correct coverage can be either by poor design or inadequate workmanship and is more common an occurrence than you would think. Back to using our spray to help support our deductions: you now understand that spraying exposed areas is not indicative of carbonation prevailing throughout all concrete. With age, carbonation naturally occurs to the upper most surface of exposed concrete and it is for this reason that the depth of reinforcement bars is subject to design best practice, outlined in the previously mentioned AS3600 for concrete structures. Typical expected depths range from at least 30mm and upwards. Therefore, the best way to undertake this test is to obtain a sample of the concrete by coring out a cylinder of it to be sent to a laboratory to be tested for their depth of carbonation. Cores need to be carefully obtained, ensuring that the sample is taken between reinforcement bars. This location can be ascertained using either reliable as-built drawings showing the exact position of reinforcement, or a concrete x-ray device can be used to locate the position and depth of the bars. Ideally both checks are made before coring out your sample.

It seems as great as concrete can be, there is a lot that goes into ensuring the reinforcement doesn't corrode since it is crucial in maintaining concrete's integrity and performance. This requires balancing numerous interrelated elements, including the initial mix ratios, types of aggregate, and additives. What if there were scenarios where you didn't have to worry so much about all those variables for concrete to perform adequately? In 2013 James Cook University in Brisbane partnered with a construction materials company to develop a unique recycled macro synthetic fibre called eMesh: recycled from 100% plastic. Representing the next generation of innovation for standard virgin plastic fibres in concrete, eMesh is a more sustainable, cost-effective, easier, and safer-to-use alternative to the conventional concrete reinforcements. Although it can't be used for all structural applications, opportunity was abound. The Cross River Rail Project in Brisbane was a massive city-wide infrastructure project which involved constructing a 10.2-kilometre rail line, 5.9 kilometres of twin tunnels running under the Brisbane River, and four new underground stations. The project featured eMesh reinforcement in its construction,[4] primarily for reinforcing concrete pavements, acting as mini reinforcing bars distributed throughout the concrete, providing effective crack control and enhancing durability. The mix design doesn't have to take into consideration the same factors it previously did, like maintaining its alkalinity for example, which was previously needed to create the passive protective layer for the reinforcement. Polypropylene fibres do not corrode and therefore don't expand causing cracking.

While the Opal Tower exemplifies failures in design and construction, the Hard Rock Hotel collapse in New Orleans reveals the deadly consequences of unapproved changes and ignored warnings. A street corner in New Orleans was the long-time home of a Woolworths store until Hurricane Katrina destroyed it in 2005.[5] It lay in ruin until eventually, Hard Rock Hotels purchased the site in 2018. Their plan was to construct a $70 million USD, steel and concrete framed, 350 room hotel. The development had got a dispensation to build higher than the zone height limit based on the business it would bring to the local area. Construction had already begun when the engineer designers made changes to already approved plans. Meanwhile, some workers kept hundreds of photos of things that didn't look right to them, including missing connections between beams and columns.[6] Investors allegedly sought additions such as penthouses with higher ceilings. Since the designers had to work within the already approved height constraints, they got creative. Documents from 2018 showed there was a decision to modify steel beams to make them thinner. The

Chapter 4: Concrete

change already exceeded the approved height by 4.5 metres, and by reducing the height of beams on floors 16-18, they reclaimed 28 centimetres from each floor. This might have worked if they had reduced the spans of the beams by adding more columns. They did not. The original plan required 11 columns, but the modifications required 24 columns. Further, the 11 columns remained undersized. As a result, the 16th floor was too heavy to be held by the structure underneath it. Metal decking which is used to pour and form up the concrete floor slabs was replaced with a lighter weight metal deck, which was also cheaper. None of these alterations were submitted to the City of New Orleans Council. By 12 October 2019, the 18th-storey slab had been poured and the stress of two storeys on top of the under designed 16th-storey was too much. Shoring props and columns failed, triggering a progressive collapse, killing three workers. Videos of the collapse captured its domino effect, starting at the 16th floor and cascading downward. This gave investigators their initial observations.

Following the disaster legal action was taken against the developer, architects, engineers, and other companies involved, alleging negligence in the design and construction processes. However, a Louisiana grand jury ultimately decided against indicting any individuals, citing insufficient evidence to meet the threshold for criminal charges.[7] The aftermath of the collapse included prolonged demolition efforts and significant disruptions in the area. The site became yet another focal point for discussions on building safety, regulatory oversight, and the responsibilities of construction professionals.

Problem solving isn't limited to proactively practicing ODEC, it can happen accidentally. These moments of inspiration are an extension of the observational stage, where unexpected connections emerge. It's one of my favourite ways to solve a problem – to stop working on it completely and go about my life (remember diffuse mode). It might be months before an ah-ha moment occurs, but if the problem isn't urgent and I'm willing to wait, I've been surprised at how often a solution will come to me when doing something else. Think of the discoveries humankind has made that were simply accidental but they solved problems because the person who discovered them happened to make a connection between apparently unrelated ideas. This is ODEC stretched out, specifically O-Observations, up to the point where D-Deductions bring the ah-ha moment, the convergence of ideas, sometimes of different worlds. Penicillin, microwave ovens, X-rays, Post-it notes and safety glass were all accidental discoveries which solved problems beyond their intended scope, often reshaping entire industries. Concrete is the second most used material in the world after water. It is responsible for the near entirety of our built environment and 8% of global greenhouse gas emissions. It turns out that's a problem that can use solving.

In 2002, David Stone was researching how to prevent iron corrosion. He didn't think his experiment worked after it started "bubbling and spitting". However, when he came in the next day he observed a "very hard, glassy" product had been created and he realised it might be useful.[8] This was the birth of Ferrock; a building material composed of waste steel dust and silica from ground up glass. It's five times stronger than Portland cement, and flexible enough to withstand movement from seismic activity. It's even stronger in salt water environments making it ideal for marine applications. As it dries it sequesters CO_2, trapping greenhouse gases in a similar way to timber, making it a carbon negative product. Whilst it's potential application is currently limited as a replacement for non-structural concrete elements, Stone continues his work to commercialise Ferrock and increase its adoption.

"I am in this for the long haul," Stone said. "Time is on our side, since, in this era of global warming unsustainable processes like cement manufacture will have to give way to greener alternatives."[9] If the problem isn't urgent and you're willing to wait… those are two variables I'm willing to bet Stone understands will inevitably change. He's solved a problem, and the market is likely to come to him sooner rather than later.

Chapter 5: Masonry

*Three bricklayers are asked what they are doing.
The first says, 'I am laying bricks.' The second
says, 'I am building a wall.' The third says, 'I am
building a cathedral.*

Sir Christopher Wren, the architect who rebuilt St. Paul's Cathedral in London after the Great Fire of 1666

Christine Foster was 26 when she left Australia to travel to Edinburgh where her father was originally from. Edinburgh is a city of contrasts: the old town, containing the Royal Mile constructed over 1,000 years ago, with medieval structures leading all the way up to Edinburgh Castle; and its Georgian new town, containing the principal shopping high street, Princes Street, containing Georgian architecture constructed between the 1700s and mid-1800s. Having lived in Edinburgh for six of my formative student years, I can attest to its general magnificence as a cultural and architectural world class city. I loved living there and if I didn't remain in Australia, it is undoubtedly where I would be right now. Edinburgh attracts people from all over the world to holiday, work and live. Christine was a mining engineer and worked as a server at a bar located in one such Georgian building, unaware that its historic charm concealed a tragic vulnerability.

The age of these buildings demands specialist knowledge for their adaptation and maintenance. Fortunately, the UK has an abundance of heritage expertise, and a flourishing career can be had. These are typically masonry structures of brick and stone; cheap, easy to produce, fire resistant materials. Mortar is used to bind masonry into a solid mass, forming up walls.

While concrete is made of cement, water, and aggregate (sand and gravel mixed in different proportions), mortar typically consists of cement, water, and lime aggregate. Lime hardens more slowly, making it more workable. It's less brittle and less prone to cracking making it an ideal polymer: derived from Greek for 'many parts'. In this case, chemically bonded links used as an adhesive for masonry. In summary, the aggregate determines the performance and therefore appropriate use. Masonry is a cohort of building materials which includes brick, block and stone adhered together in various forms using mortar.

In the early evening of 29 June 2000, Christine was serving customers drinks at their table outside the bar when a shower of masonry suddenly claimed her life. The enquiry into her death remains unresolved more than 20 years later. The incident triggered an enquiry conducted in the Scottish Courts and took a further two years to reach a determination. The full judgement is available on the Scottish Courts and Tribunal's website[1] and shows ODEC in action.

The enquiry's determination was made by Sheriff Court, Charles Stoddard, who set about outlining his observations, beginning with the detail of the circumstances causing Christine's death. What struck her was a large stone element, quickly followed by a series of coping stones.

Imagine a straight stone wall topped off with a series of flat stones. This topping or capping is referred to as coping stones. They prevent rainwater from getting inside the wall and are adhered to the top of the wall on a bed of mortar. Now imagine this wall, but at roof level and at a 45-degree angle. To complete this roof ridge common to Georgian buildings, imagine another larger stone

Chapter 5: Masonry

located at the bottom of the ridge, sitting on top of the building's wall, receiving the load from the weight of the roof ridge and it's coping stones. This is referred to in the determination as the knee stone. It is often a decorative feature but it's primary function is to project outward, 'catching' the bottom of the ridge line. This knee stone failed, breaking off to fall to the ground. Apparently with no mortar bedding holding them down, the coping stones also slid down the ridge line falling to the ground.

The questions brought forth by this observation, like why did the knee stone break and why were the coping stones not properly adhered to their bed, rely on methodical investigation for clear answers. Using a structured process like ODEC, the court examined each potential cause, such as workmanship quality, weather conditions, and vibrations, testing these hypotheses against the available evidence. This systematic elimination of possibilities allowed the court to piece together the most probable explanation for the failure.

Attention was drawn to refurbishment works that were undertaken to the roof some eleven years before the tragedy, making the possible cause a question of workmanship. The implied deduction is: the performance of coping stones adhered to a mortar bed required adequate workmanship. The coping stones were not adhered properly and slid down the ridge. Therefore, inadequate workmanship caused the coping stones to slide down the ridge.

Contributing to the enquiry's observations, further evidence was spoken in. Including:

- Confirmation of the prevailing weather conditions at the time leading up to, and during the incident;
- Photographs taken of the subject property by a tourist staying opposite just four days before the incident;
- Results received from vibration monitoring equipment demonstrating the effect of vibrations potentially caused by vehicle traffic, which features frequent bus movements immediately adjacent the property;
- The possible effect of vibration from works undertaken to the front of the building in 1991, which included the use of percussion drilling;
- Interpretations of the observations by an expert witness, a Chartered Civil Engineer; and
- A statement from the Chartered Quantity Surveyor who acted as the cost consultant on the 1988-90 refurbishment contract, testifying that no proper account was taken of the potential for seasonal expansion and contraction of lead flashing.

Additional deductions are formulated from these observations, such as the force of wind loosened the mortar holding the coping stones, or perhaps the mortar was vibrated loose, either by neighbouring traffic or power tools. One by one, each was eliminated through close examination and scrutiny. For example, consider this excerpt from the Sheriff Court's determination:

Chapter 5: Masonry

... evidence from Alan France, a Chartered Quantity Surveyor and the Cost Consultant on the 1988-90 contract that when fixing an excessive amount of the lead flashing on the wall head no proper account was taken of the potential for seasonal expansion and contraction. This might, itself, have led to a loosening of the mortar bond. Mr Coll for the Council asked me to accept this evidence and to include a finding to that effect; but none of this was put to the three engineers who considered in detail the failure mechanism. Without better and stronger evidence, I do not consider this alleged failure to be established, although it is a possibility.

He acknowledges it is a *possibility* but doesn't hang his hat on it. He can't "without better and stronger evidence". This does not eliminate the possibility, but it's not possible to draw a conclusion.

The Sheriff Court concluded that he had sufficient evidence that proved a lack of, or inadequate mortar (he described it as a gap) which was supposed to hold the line of coping stones in place. They had slipped, placing an additional load onto the knee stone that it wasn't designed for, causing the knee stone to fail and it all to fall to the ground. For the purposes of the enquiry, it "satisfies that test". Ultimately, those who had been responsible for fixing the coping stones to the wall head during the 1988-90 contract had used 'shoddy' workmanship. Shoddy is a distinctly British word repeated throughout the determination, meaning poor or inadequate in this case. Christine's death might have been avoided if those renovating the wall head in 1988-90 had used proper workmanship.

At approximately 3:30am on 1 May 2023, sandstone blocks fell from the parapet of a former bank building in Thurso, Scotland. No one was injured likely owing to the fact the failure occurred before most people were awake. The risk of falling materials from period properties remains elevated in excess of twenty years after Christine's death. The Scottish Parliamentary Working Group on the Maintenance of Tenement Scheme Property has been meeting since March 2018 and in 2019 published three recommendations including five yearly inspections, establishing compulsory sinking funds and owners associations.[2] These are supported by Scottish Government and currently being reviewed by Scottish Law Commission. Legislation is expected by 2026.

****

A critical aspect of heritage buildings is their plasterwork, which tells its own story of adaptation and innovation. How do you accurately identify and age a plaster ceiling? Understanding Australia's role in the history of plasterwork used throughout the world today holds the answer.

Decorations made from plaster in New South Wales (NSW) have their history between 1788 and 1939. The earliest known plaster cornice in Australia is 1816 in The Mint, Macquarie Street, Sydney.[3] In colonial Australia, a lack of limestone was a major disadvantage, not just for decorative plaster, but just to make mortar to hold stone and brick buildings together. With no limestone to mine, sea shells with a similar composition were found and burned. However, there was no substitute for gypsum. In England lime plaster was used - made from limestone and gypsum - for decorative plasterwork. It was cost-prohibitive to import into Australia, as other economic challenges restricted imports to essential goods only. That changed in the 1830s when NSW experienced their first economic boom and luxury goods were imported for the first time. The lack of skilled craftspeople up to around 1840s, together with climate and mode of living, made the use of decorative plaster both inaccessible and inconsistent.

The 1850s saw an increase in migrants and with it an increase in demand for middle income housing. This encouraged plasterers to look for an alternative material to lime. Rather than sculpting by hand, in 1858 gelatine was used to create moulds in which the existing materials could be moulded into with increased efficiency and accuracy. Due to the proliferation of gelatine moulds, from the 1860s the variety of decorations increased and so did demand on modelers. Another building boom compelled the plastering industry

Chapter 5: Masonry

to look for a material which would allow them to produce faster and cheaper. They looked to England again for the answer and found it in canvas plaster, also known as rag, stick and fibrous plaster. Canvas plaster decorations were made by reinforcing plaster with layers of canvas. This technique strengthened the material while reducing the amount of plaster needed, lowering costs. The first use of canvas plaster decorations was in the YMCA building in Sydney in 1885. The 1880s is regarded as the "golden age" of Australian decorative plasterwork, following which pre-decorated metal ceilings began to rise, rivalling fibrous plaster panels.

In response to the now decrease in demand for their work, modelers once again looked to innovate. They considered replacing canvas plaster, experimenting with various additives, including straw, sugar cane (also referred to as bagasse, manufactured under the name Bagasse), and cotton wool.

George Augustine Taylor was a cartoonist, inventor and publisher of several journals including *Building*: the magazine for the architect, builder, property owner & merchant. Around 1900 he invented and produced his own fibrous plaster for a new company he formed with merchant Alexander Knox. Taylor patented a new improved type of fibrous plaster for ornamental use on ceilings, walls, cornices and even temporary outdoor structures. It was first used to construct the Citizen's Arch in Sydney during Federation celebrations in 1901[4] but soon after installed in many commercial and domestic buildings.

Canvas reinforced plaster that could be produced in moulds became popular in Australia from the 1880s as it was cheaper and less likely to crack than normal gypsum-based plaster. In the late 19th and early 20th centuries, several Australian companies experimented with making even lighter and stronger plaster by adding new elements like wood shavings, straw, millet, grass or wool. Taylor's improved fibrous plaster contained bagasse, a by-product of the sugarcane refining process and he subsequently named his company after this material. It proved to be inexpensive, durable, easily moulded and, according to Taylor, it could be cut or punctured without cracking, unlike most other plaster. The first true fibrous plaster was made in 1912 in West Richmond, Victoria: a layer of plaster reinforced by a layer of teased hemp and sealed with a second layer of plaster. This was rapidly adopted throughout Australia until 1920s, when it was then copied by America and Britain. Today 'plaster glass' is made of plaster, which has been reinforced by either horsehair, copra fibre, hemp, coconut or glass fibre. The plaster glass panel is then secured in place by hessian straps to the ceiling's timber framing. The use of additives as a binding agent in plaster goes as far back as medieval times in England. Animal hair additives can give rise to the risk of anthrax, a type of potentially fatal bacterial infection, which can remain dormant for hundreds of years. Anthrax cases are rare, with only 17 human cases in the UK since 1981 and no fatalities.[5] However, surveyors and tradespeople inspecting heritage buildings with historic plaster should remain mindful of this potential risk of exposure.

It's clear the history of plasterwork is a great example of innovation being driven by necessity; in this case, by cycles in economic demand within a fledgling colonisation, followed by an urgency to maintain relevance and competitiveness. The use of gelatine moulds is a non-obvious creative solution, where naturally one defaults their thinking to the status quo, as in replacing materials like-for-like, without considering an entirely different approach. Eventually, the conditions led to the method of historic plasterwork that can be observed in countries like the UK and the USA today.

Finally, two world wars devastated the plastering industry. Although a large deposit of gypsum was discovered in South Australia, only a small amount of Australian plaster of Paris was ever made due to a lack of an established industry. The War progressed and the market for decorative plasterwork vanished, many modelling firms closed their doors for good.

Plaster was ultimately born from the derivative processes required to construct masonry, with its beginnings rooted in the versatility of

Chapter 5: Masonry

lime. Plaster glass ceilings remain present in public buildings and domestic homes today, especially prevalent in Western Australia. When speculating a house purchase, a diligent buyer will see that their pre-purchase inspection report makes comment on its status since dirt buildup over time will result in a sagging ceiling and increased risk of failure. As plaster glass ceilings are held in place by hessian straps, over the course of their life, re-strapping may be required. Ensuring regular maintenance of plaster glass ceilings mitigates issues. In 2015 a five-year-old boy was taken to hospital with minor injuries when part of a ceiling caved in at a Western Australian primary school in February 2015.[6] Other failures followed, well publicising the Department's response, which included their cyclical program to re-inspect ceilings as part of the overall building inspections at public schools on a three yearly basis.[7]

Be aware of anyone that can repair your plaster glass ceilings by re-screwing. Plaster glass ceilings should never be re-screwed as this is not how they were installed. The screw will break through the plaster glass ceiling sheeting due to the weight and the construction of the plasterglass board. Screws are only designed for use on gypsum-based plasterboard panels, also known as gypsum board or drywall, where plaster is held in place between two sheets of paper.

****

Following 1871, Chicago was a city on the rise, recovering from the Great Fire and booming with architectural innovation. Amidst this backdrop, the Monadnock Building emerged as a symbol of engineering prowess and architectural evolution. Designers, John Wellborn Root and Daniel Burnham, did not explicitly set out to create the tallest brick building in the world. However, the height of the Monadnock Building in Chicago, became a significant aspect of its design due to the economic and architectural ambitions of its developers, Peter and Shepherd Brooks. The building was named after Mount Monadnock in New Hampshire, reflecting the Brooks brothers' admiration for the mountain's enduring strength and simplicity. Constructed in 1893, it is considered to be the tallest load-bearing masonry building in the world. This means it is a habitable building with multiple floors, where the walls themselves bear the structural load of the building, which transfer down 16-storeys to a granite base. It tapers off towards the top, demonstrating the height limitations of traditional masonry construction. The building was an immediate success, quickly becoming fully occupied. Its simplicity and strength symbolised a new direction in architectural design, emphasising functionality and structural integrity. The structural innovations required for its construction highlighted the limitations of masonry for tall buildings and spurred the development and adoption of a much lighter building material: steel. In 1893, the south half of the Monadnock was constructed using a steel frame. While the south half retained the visual simplicity of the north, it included more modern amenities and larger windows, highlighting the transition from load-bearing masonry to steel-frame construction in high-rise buildings. The architects and builders pushed the boundaries of what was possible, and ultimately laid the groundwork for the skyscrapers that now define city skylines around the world.

While Monadnock represents the height of masonry innovation, the road from the birth of masonry by homo-sapiens reaches as far back as 11,500 years, to one of the earliest known examples of masonry techniques in construction used to build Göbekli Tepe in Turkey[8], a series of stone structures and pillars. We've been constructing for a long time. Any early innovations are simply lost to the dark ages. For instance, we still don't fully understand the exact methods used to quarry, transport, and erect Stonehenge in England, or the Moai statues on Easter Island. Experimental archaeology has provided some insights, but definitive evidence is lacking, and they remain archaeological enigmas. Inside the last thousand years however, there is something to be learned. From Chicago to the Philippines, masonry techniques have evolved across the globe, shaped by local needs and materials. Following their discovery of a set of islands in 1521, Spanish colonisers introduced advanced masonry techniques

Chapter 5: Masonry

to the Philippines during their 333-year rule, which significantly shaped the country's architectural heritage. They built structures like churches, forts, and bridges using masonry construction, blending European techniques with vernacular materials. This period saw the creation of the iconic building archetype, the bahay na bato (ba·hay-na-ba·to), Filipino for "stone house".[9] Bahay na bato are houses which are an upgraded version of the Bahay kubo, or Nipa hut, the nipa being a type of abundantly available palm. It was designed to address the country's problem caused by natural events such as earthquakes and typhoons. Bahay na bato combined adobe walls with wooden upper levels and a nipa roof. Adobe is a building material made from earth and organic materials, such as straw. They are bricks traditionally made by mixing mud and straw, forming the mixture into bricks, and drying them in the sun. These bricks are then used to build walls, which are typically thick and possess excellent thermal mass, helping to keep buildings cool in hot climates and warm in colder conditions. Adobe construction is an ancient technique commonly used in arid regions around the world due to its insulation properties and availability of materials. A cob wall is similar to an adobe wall, save one key difference: while adobe are bricks which are dried in the sun, cob is built in situ by layering and sculpting a wet mixture directly into the wall without forming bricks. Nipa is strategically used as a roof covering so when a typhoon hits, the easily replaceable roof is designed to be blown off, whilst the structure remains intact. Bahay na bato's architectural style represented a fusion of Spanish and indigenous Filipino craftsmanship, contributing to the country's cultural heritage. Spanish masonry techniques left a lasting physical imprint on the built environment. These techniques which focus on using local materials and ancient methods are still in practice today. Community elders recognise that modern techniques are not sustainable and more expensive, so they continue to teach the 'old ways'.

Chapter 6: Timber

The older the problem, the older the solution.

Naval Ravikant

Nearly a thousand years ago, in the year 1163, a bishop in Paris commenced construction of a new cathedral. Pope Alexander III laid the first stone and over a hundred years later the building was completed.

Notre-Dame de Paris is constructed primarily from masonry (limestone, in this case). Stone built angled support columns and beams, called flying buttresses, are used to support the heavy limestone walls of the large towers while still allowing space for giant rose glass and stained-glass windows. Limestone, indeed, masonry generally, is a heavy construction material, which had 13th century limitations. Yet, the central space down the middle of the cathedral, the nave, reached an unusually high 35 metres. Over six hundred years before Monadnock was constructed, builders already knew how to make Notre-Dame taller still: A lighter weight material was used to construct the roof and spire.

The word "wood" refers to trees that have not yet experienced any sort of intervention. Timber refers to a period in a tree's life after it has been cut down, including crushed trees used in construction and architecture, cellulose fibres or pulpwood used in paper manufacturing, and so on. Constructed from timber, Notre-Dame's first spire was built around 1250. By 1786 it had deteriorated, further exacerbated by wind loads, posing a risk of materials falling onto people below, so it was dismantled. In 1844 a 30-year-old architect was commissioned to restore the cathedral finally replacing the missing spire to the timber roof.[1] It eventually received the nickname, "the forest", because of how dense and intricate the spire's timber construction was.[2] The cathedral experienced great adversity in its life showing incredible resilience. It survived the French revolution and World War II. That is until 15 April 2019 when it succumbed to a fire completely destroying the timber roof and spire in broad daylight before thousands of onlookers.

This event triggered two investigations unrelated to each other, but with the cathedral at their core. An investigation into the circumstances which caused the fire and subsequent accountability; and the transformation of Notre-Dame into a living laboratory providing researchers an unprecedented opportunity to understand construction techniques of the past. The restoration project was not only focused on rebuilding the cathedral but also on preserving its historical and cultural significance. An interdisciplinary approach included historians, archaeologists, architects, and engineers working together. Their common goal was to use modern scientific techniques to uncover more about the cathedral's past while ensuring its future.

The use of timber in the construction of Notre-Dame has baffled the studiers of the cathedral for decades. Although much of the cathedral, especially the roof, is timber, there has never been a case of insect infestation or weakening of the structure. While the majority of the timber did burn during the fire many pieces were barely damaged. For the first time, timber from the cathedral was taken down and studied. It was found that the timber primarily used was oak, and of exceptionally high quality. Oak is known for its durability and resistance to pests. The trees selected for construction

Chapter 6: Timber

were mature and well-seasoned, which reduced their susceptibility to insect damage.

During restoration efforts, researchers uncovered large iron staples holding together the cathedral's stone blocks. In light of this unexpected discovery, Notre-Dame became the first known Gothic cathedral to make such extensive use of iron as a construction material. Wall ties to be exact, like those used in modern cavity brick walls. Dating and metallurgical analyses revealed that these iron reinforcements date back to the first construction phase of the church in the 12th century. But more importantly, the mystery of why the nave was able to reach its 35-metre height in the first place, was solved.

The first spire was taken down in the 1700s because it was no longer structurally sound. During the post-Hugo renovations of the 1800s another spire was added. It was this secondary spire that was constructed using the wood from over 52 acres of forest. Over 2,000 pieces of timber remained from the fire. Scientists believed that through studying it they could pinpoint where the logs were cut from, when they were cut, how they were grown and how old the trees were when they were harvested for the spire. The lead used in the structure doesn't provide this ability because it can melt and re-harden over time which interferes with identifying the age of the material.

As for the circumstances which caused the fire, Notre-Dame was undergoing extensive renovation work when the fire was ignited and soon after the investigation commenced, workers confessed to smoking on the scaffolding. DNA tests completed on cigarette butts found this to be the case. However, the fire started *inside* the cathedral, and no one was able to confirm if anyone smoked inside. The next hypothesis related to electrical wiring located in the roof, contemplating that a short circuit occurred creating the fire's source of ignition. The Paris public prosecutor's office released their preliminary findings two months after the fire, "favouring the theory of an accident".[3]

The Building Detective

After five years of restoration works, the cathedral reopened its doors to the world in December 2024. Fire-prevention features, such as a sprinkler system and fire compartmentalisation, formed part of restoration efforts. These types of fire safety systems were not previously installed and would have prevented or likely minimised the disaster.

****

Austria has a long-standing tradition of forestry and woodworking, with forests covering nearly half of the country.[4] Austrian researchers and engineers were motivated by the growing need for sustainable building materials and during the 1990s, there was an increasing awareness of the environmental impact of traditional construction materials like concrete and steel. Professionals recognised that trees, being a renewable resource, had the potential to serve as a more sustainable alternative. For larger, taller buildings traditional timber construction methods faced limitations in terms of structural stability. Engineers sought to overcome these challenges by engineering timber products that could provide the necessary strength and stability. Working closely with other researchers, universities, and industry partners in Austria and Switzerland, these teams developed the process of bonding layers of timber at right angles to each other using structural adhesives such as polyurethane and formaldehyde. This crosswise arrangement not only enhanced the strength and stability of the panels but also minimised timber's natural expansion and contraction due to moisture changes. This product is called cross laminated timber, or CLT. A manufacturer named KLH opened the world's first cross-laminated timber plant in Katsch, Austria, in 1999.[5]

CLT has caught on as a sort of catch all term, or industry buzzword, to describe a whole building constructed using this material, however CLT buildings comprise various components which include Glulam or GLT: Glue laminated timber. Glulam is made by gluing together multiple layers of timber with the grains of all layers running *parallel* to each other. These are used for beams, columns,

Chapter 6: Timber

arches, and curved structures due to its high strength and versatility. Meanwhile, CLT's layers run *perpendicular* to each other, and are used for walls, floors, ceilings and roofs. Altogether a structure built using the majority of these materials is called a mass timber structure. The term "hybrid" in mass timber construction refers to combining different building materials to create a structure that leverages the strengths of each material. Hybrid systems often integrate mass timber elements like CLT and GLT with other materials such as steel and concrete. These combinations are used to create gravity framing systems; structural components that support the building's weight and transfer loads to the foundation.

Ten short years after KLH opened their plant in Austria, they supplied the materials for the world's first high-density, residential, mass timber building, Stadthaus, London in 2009.[6] Austrian organisations actively promoted mass timber through industry events, publications, and training programs, raising awareness and building expertise within the construction sector. Not only did Austria export mass timber products to international markets but also shared their expertise and technology with other countries, helping to establish mass timber as a viable construction method worldwide.

In 2018, Brisbane opened Australia's largest engineered mass timber building, "25 King", standing at 10-storeys tall or 52 metres in height, one of the tallest in the world. It's used as an open plan office complex and pushes the boundaries of what the Australian construction industry thought was possible from mass timber construction. Timber provides excellent natural insulation, which contributes to the building's energy efficiency by reducing heating and cooling costs. The manufacturing and construction processes for timber have lower embodied energy than those for steel and concrete. Incorporating natural materials like timber into building design is part of the biophilic design trend, which aims to connect occupants more closely with nature and reduce sick building syndrome. Studies have shown that environments with natural materials like timber can reduce stress, improve mood, and enhance overall well-being. Not everyone, however, is readily accepting that mass timber construction is the answer to our sustainability and well-being goals.

World-leading fire safety expert Professor José Torero has expressed his concern about the adoption speed of mass timber construction.[7] Torero argues that mass timber buildings are being adopted too rapidly without a corresponding increase in the competency of architects and engineers working with the material. He believes that many professionals lack sufficient experience and knowledge about the unique fire safety challenges posed by mass timber, leading to potential design and construction deficiencies. Even though timber has beneficial charring properties that can slow burn rate, it's still a combustible material. In large and tall buildings, a fire could spread more rapidly and potentially cause more significant damage than in buildings made of non-combustible materials like concrete or steel. Torero fears that a major fire in a timber building could not only destroy the structure but also endanger surrounding buildings. Furthermore, the combustion of certain adhesives can release toxic gases. Polyurethane adhesives, in particular, can emit hazardous substances like hydrogen cyanide and carbon monoxide when burned. Phenol-resorcinol-formaldehyde adhesives release toxic formaldehyde gas when burned.

Torero calls for a comprehensive, science-based approach to fire safety that specifically addresses the unique properties of mass timber. Without rigorous standards and thorough understanding, there is a risk that these buildings could be vulnerable to catastrophic fire events. Any significant fire incident in a mass-timber building could lead to a knee-jerk regulatory response, potentially restricting or even banning the use of mass timber. With all of this said, Torero states that timber is perfectly safe, if done right. Specifications for standardised assemblies which have been subject to a full fire test help ensure performance and compliance. When inspecting a mass timber building, the building detective

Chapter 6: Timber

should keep their eyes peeled for any signs of warping, shrinkage, or fungal growth, as well as fastener integrity: the condition and quality of fasteners such as bolts and screws. Signs of corrosion or loosening could be indicative of compromised structural stability.

****

At around 1am on 2 September 1666, a bakery on Pudding Lane which supplied bread to the royal court of King Charles II, caught fire. A strong easterly wind rapidly spread the flames to nearby timber and thatch homes. It had been an unusually long, dry summer, and so the closely packed timber buildings, along with their thatched roofs were very dry indeed. The fire raged, and initial attempts to control it included demolishing houses to create firebreaks, but these efforts were delayed and insufficient. The Lord Mayor of London, Sir Thomas Bloodworth, initially underestimated the severity of the fire, reportedly saying, "Pish! A woman could piss it out." It appears that even though politicians have managed to find the constitutional will to update legislation over hundreds of years, the same might not be said for the way they talk today. Moving on.

The Great Fire of London ultimately destroyed a significant portion of the city, including 87 churches, 13,200 houses, and numerous public buildings. What followed was the Rebuilding Act of 1667, which introduced regulations to prohibit timber construction, and to ensure buildings from that point forward were constructed with brick or stone. Before then the only major area built with brick or stone was the wealthy centre of the city, where the mansions of the merchants and brokers stood on spacious lots. Present day legislation contains the legacy of the fire and continues to influence contemporary building regulations in London and beyond. However, with the construction of the mass timber Stadthaus, it's not as though the ban on timber construction was suddenly lifted after 342 years. Various key developments and advances took place during that period that paved the way for changes in building practices, such as the industrial revolution following which steel and concrete became more common. By the 20th century advances in fireproofing and construction materials allowed for flexibility in building codes. There is a delicate balance between trial and error, but it is hard to ignore that it takes catastrophe for policy, regulation and legislation to finally come all too quickly and all too late.

Driven by the material's sustainability, seismic resilience, and efficiency in construction, Japan has also seen growing adoption of CLT since around 2012. Osaka hosted Expo 2025, for which a five-storey, ring-shaped mass timber pavilion was constructed. The use of mass timber in both public and private sector projects is redefining modern timber construction in Japan. Traditional Japanese timber construction has a history that stretches back over 1,400 years. The earliest known examples of Japanese timber construction can be traced to the Asuka period (538–710 AD), with structures such as the Hōryū-ji temple complex, dating back to around 607 AD.[8] Traditional Japanese buildings often use post-and-beam construction, known as *minka*, for residential structures and *machiya*, for urban townhouses. These structures rely on a framework of vertical posts and horizontal beams, often joined without nails using intricate wooden joinery techniques like mortise and tenon joints.

Iconic structures like temples (*tera*) and shrines (*jinja*) are masterpieces of timber construction, showcasing advanced carpentry skills and the use of large timber components. A master joiner or carpenter need not lament that they were not present hundreds of years ago to provide their contribution; in fact, every twenty years Ise Grand Shrine is carefully dismantled and then rebuilt. A practice that has endured for the last 1,300 years.[9] Further, it is rebuilt using specially grown trees. Some of the timber used for the Ise Shrine must be of a certain size, a role fulfilled only by *hinoki* trees (Japanese Cypress) more than two hundred years old. The rebuilding of the Ise Shrine involves the meticulous work of master carpenters who use traditional joinery techniques without nails or metal fasteners. This method, known as *kanawatsugi*,

Chapter 6: Timber

requires precision and expertise to create joints that fit perfectly and can withstand the test of time. Carpenters pass down their tools and techniques through generations, ensuring that the knowledge and skills required for this work remain alive and vibrant.

Traditional timber buildings in Japan incorporate flexibility and shock absorption to withstand earthquakes. Features like braced frames (*tokyo*) and sliding panels (*fusuma*) help distribute seismic forces. If you are a modern building inspector in Japan and you find yourself inspecting ancient temples and shrines, it's comforting to know that your toolkit is surprisingly the same; the detective is still on the lookout for any clues indicating decay, rot, insect activity, cracks, compromised fasteners and moisture damage.

Preserving heritage is a practice of various western countries that's supported by rules and regulations. In most places, you can't just do whatever you want without getting planning approvals first, nor are buildings routinely dismantled and rebuilt. Whilst specific buildings enjoy the protection of heritage status, conservation areas in the UK expand similar protection very generally to a wide area to manage and protect the special architectural and historic interest of a place. Every local authority in England has at least one conservation area, and there are around 10,000 in England.[10] Generally, what all of this means is stuff looks the same. Rows of houses have consistent character.

Whilst Australia has heritage controls in place for specific buildings or even just the odd façade here and there, when it comes to residential housebuilding in suburbia there is no such uniformity. Look upon any populated hillside and you will see a patchwork quilt of steel sheet roofing in a range of colours between lush, subtropical flora. Homes in Australia come in all shapes and sizes but Queensland is home to one of Australia's oldest, most consistent and recognisable forms of housing: the timber constructed Queenslander.

The Building Detective

The traditional Queenslander homes were constructed between 1880 and 1920. It's possible that no one alive today has built an authentic Queenslander, although there is no shortage of contemporary attempts to replicate their charm. It is a quadrilateral timber house raised off the ground, which has a balcony or veranda wrapped around it, and a hipped roof on all four sides. Being timber, there are many decorative characteristics that feature above the internal doors, to cornices and verandah handrails. From a construction perspective, key features of a Queenslander reflect the time in which they were conceived. They include:

- timber-frame construction: where there was a local abundance of quality softwood;
- exposed structural framing and studs: this represents an economic use of materials and enables easier relocation due to reduced weight;
- perimeter balconies or verandas: sheltering protects the house from both direct sunlight and torrential downpours; and
- being raised on stumps: promoted ventilation in the humid climate and an easier way to monitor for termites.

When settlers first constructed Queenslanders they were typically on leasehold land; land they paid someone else to live on, so the ability to take their home with them was important. The transportability of a Queenslander is something that endures today as a modern feature. Owning a Queenslander means you don't have to part with it but can simply have it moved to a new location. It can be faster and cheaper than building a new home and arguably the unique character is not easily replicated.

Another important consideration when surveying Queenslanders is termites. Termites are not fond of natural light and, if exposed to it or the open air, they will dehydrate and die. They therefore build mud tunnels over hard objects rather than emerge. These tubes, or galleries, are made up of partly digested timber and excreted mud and are moist if in active use. Termites keep their colony nest and

Chapter 6: Timber

galleries at 25–35°C and enjoy high humidity. They live in constant darkness except during the summer, when swarms of winged reproductive termites take flight. Given the timber-frame construction, it is essential for a professional pest controller to adhere to the requirements for inspections and reports set out in local standards. This will help correctly identify the species found in a property. Some species of termites will not attack dry-seasoned timbers in a building, while others can be highly destructive in a short amount of time. All types of home in built-up urban areas are at risk, especially if there is a typical termite habitat nearby, such as a well-established gum tree within a 100-metre radius – a common sight in Australian suburbia. Termite colony development is also encouraged by automatic watering systems, landscaping, maintenance and inappropriate design that allows hidden entry into a building. If the presence of termites is identified, they are not to be disturbed. Should they be shaken up, they will often abandon the area and move on to cause damage in other parts of the building. In the early days of Queenslander construction, settlers attempted to deal with termites using hot tar, castor oil and arsenic[11] – often without much success. In a few cases, therefore, it may be possible to identify soil that has been contaminated. Annual inspections, improving ventilation, and removing timber in contact with soil are key to minimising termite risk. Today, an approved chemical soil treatment is used around the building perimeter (referred to as the treated zone) and within the subfloor, to eradicate termites trying to gain entry.

In limited circumstances, particularly in areas where there is live termite activity, bait stations are installed and monitored. This method relies heavily on the insect finding and consuming sufficient bait and returning to the nest without entering the property, however.

Metal plates on top of stumps to create an overhang or drip, are called ant-caps. These can restrict the access of termites into the building as well, but they don't render it entirely pest-proof. They act as a deterrent because termites don't favour creating their galleries upside down, and if they are successful, they become easier to identify. When the building is affected by rot, a Queenslander can make the ideal environment for termites to thrive. Generally speaking, then, termite risk reduction measures include improving subfloor ventilation, removal of timber in contact with the soil, and improving access areas for inspection.

It would be almost professionally irresponsible of me if I didn't touch on the topic of timber rot before wrapping up a chapter on timber aimed at problem solvers. Distinct from insect attack, for which you can readily find identification guides online that go well beyond termites, there are generally speaking two forms of rot that you should be aware of: wet and dry.

The word rot is used as a noun and a verb. As a verb it describes the action of wood deteriorating due to fungal infection. Wet rot is the more common fungi affecting wood and timber, where affected areas present as dark, soft and spongy. The vegetative part of the fungus might also be visible, called mycelium. This is a network of fine white filaments (hyphae) used by the fungus to absorb nutrients from their environment. In areas affected by wet rot, the mycelium may be visible as white or yellow. All rot (and this is the noun), and mould, require three conditions to thrive: the right moisture, the right temperature, and something to eat. For wet rot this is a moisture content greater than 40%, a temperature greater than 30°C and the sustenance is generally a wood type that is not resistant to rot or is untreated.

Dry rot is less common, but far more insidious than wet rot. It is something I've seen with my own eyes only once in my career, in a disused Mancunian basement. Dry rot is a different type of fungus to wet rot, going by the name Serpula lacrymans. Remember, it needs three things to thrive: moisture, temperature and something to eat. In the case of dry rot, it technically also needs still air. Whilst this is a condition which enables the temperature and moisture, dry rot's fruiting bodies rely on the still air for reproduction. Why?

Chapter 6: Timber

Because these fleshy, pancake-like aliens explosively release their spores, dispersing them into the surrounding air. The biggest fruiting body I saw was the same size as my head, sitting in the middle of a stair tread. For a badly affected space, a layer of red/orange dust can be found on anything and everything. For the spores to germinate and start a new infection, they require a moisture content in the wood of around 20-30% and thrive in temperatures between 20°C to 25°C. If a space is not ventilated at all, then it can create these ideal conditions, and an absent draught won't interfere with the dust-like spores doing their thing. That is unless there's *just enough* of a draft to spread the spores to a comfortable new location whilst all other conditions remain the same. Oh, and the spores don't need to land on wood. They will happily feed off carpet, plaster, brick and masonry. If you have dry rot that has got out of hand, you do not have a fun problem to solve. Addressing dry rot involves systematic elimination. Halt its reproductive cycle through ventilation, fungicidal treatment, and monitoring to prevent recurrence. Most of all, proactivity is required to make sure it is gone for good.

Chapter 7: Movement

Give me a lever long enough and a fulcrum on which to place it, and I shall move the world.

Archimedes

2008 saw the completion of Mascot Towers; a residential development comprising two 10-storey residential towers, ground floor retail tenancies like grocery stores and coffee shops, all constructed above an underground train station. It was delivered by a builder on behalf of their developer client, the former City of Botany Bay Council. The certifiers acting on behalf of the council issued an occupation certificate (OC) on 1 July 2008. A valid OC is a requirement before occupying or using a new building. It means that the building has been independently checked for safety and compliance and is in line with approved construction documents.

Three years later, the body corporate for the Mascot Towers apartment complex recorded cracking observations in their meeting minutes for the first time,[1] as well as leaking water observed in the car wash bay. They agreed to appoint a consultant to investigate the defects (at the cost of owner occupiers who pay an annual levy to the body corporate for the maintenance of common property). The consultant undertook their investigation, and being diligent, identified more serious defects, including evidence of structural movement, swimming pool leaks, faulty fire systems, and defective garden irrigation systems. By 2015 the original builder made a deal with the body corporate. In the spirit of cooperation, they agreed to repair the defects identified by the consultant's report. Furthermore, the building managers accepted $750,000 AUD from the builder to waive any responsibility for ongoing defects.[2] By 2016, the City of Botany Bay Council was amalgamated with the neighbouring City of Rockdale to form Bayside Council.

Eleven years since the construction of Mascot Towers, residents received a letter from the body corporate on 13 June 2019. It acknowledged temporary props installed inside the car park and announced that they would all have to evacuate by 9pm the next day. Cracking was everywhere: to mortar joints in brickwork piers, to concrete slabs, movement joints, and blockwork perimeter walls in the car park. It was characterised as being "rapid". Temporary accommodation included a shelter set up at Mascot Town Hall.

A neighbouring apartment complex was completed directly next door, which the residents quickly alleged vibration from their construction caused catastrophic damage to their homes. A reasonable correlation to make (but the causation unable to be proven). Even though the neighbouring developer undertook a condition report of Mascot Towers prior to commencing their own work, which shows cracks existed prior, they reached an out of court settlement. The registered entity used by the original builder to deliver Mascot Towers was liquidated and no longer exists. Eventually, the majority of owners agreed to a deal, giving them a share of the $30 million AUD building price, with support from the NSW government. While the deal eliminates debts, owners will remain at a loss. It's debatable if rectification is viable. Sixteen years on, it reached a point in its lifecycle that properties aren't supposed to reach for some sixty years from completion: the end of its economic life, where demolition and redevelopment may yield a greater return than any other option.

Chapter 7: Movement

All this and the exact cause remains a mystery. Perhaps it has been covered up by millions of dollars in out of court settlements between private parties. Building detectives are left only to speculate as to the exact cause, which if known would submit yet another case study to the records, another cautionary tale, and likely further evidence to throw on the pile supporting the case for industry compliance reform. Indeed, both incidents at Opal Tower and Mascot Towers contributed to the eventual reforms to the construction industry in New South Wales (NSW), Australia, with NSW passing the Design and Building Practitioners Act (NSW) in 2020, which included a register for construction professionals and compliance declaration requirements. In May 2022, the NSW Government announced the commissioning of an investigative report into the former Botany Bay Council's handling of the whole thing. Issued on 21 March 2023 the report focused on process rather than determine any technical causes.[3] Don't forget, the original builder already paid to dissolve its risk, and then just to be sure, dissolved its company, a likely special purpose vehicle to protect them against this very scenario.

Movement in a building is normal. Buildings move! They are moved by ground conditions and the weather. They move when temperature makes materials expand and contract. And they are prepared to move in concert with a seismic event. And so, they are designed to move. Even settlement is expected following completing construction, where a building's weight fully settles into its geological foundation over the course of four changing seasons. Hairline cracks, very thin cracks that are no cause for concern, begin to appear at junctions and connections between materials, through mortar joints in brick and blockwork, and in paintwork concealing abutments between plasterboard sheets forming your internal walls or ceilings. These are closed up, sealed, plastered, repainted, and monitored. If the cracks relapse, it may call for a control joint to be installed to tidy things up. Buildings even breathe, just as your chest moves up and down when you breathe. Movement joints are installed at regular intervals in brick walls and concrete slabs to facilitate these kinds of movements.

What isn't normal are sudden cracks, and certainly openings, which indicate too much movement. A rudimentary rule of thumb to consider before becoming too alarmed is if your crack is less than 5 millimetres, get it checked out, sure, but it's unlikely to be a costly and persisting issue. If the crack you discover is an opening greater than 5 millimetres, perhaps you don't need to evacuate, but make it a priority to investigate further. Too much movement is the kind of movement where the building is not designed to move that far, this way or that way, and as a consequence, loads are not being distributed correctly risking compromising other elements that were not designed to do certain things. How much movement is too much? Well, that depends. Is the property a single-storey bungalow or a super high-rise tower? In 2017 I visited Taipei 101, a 100-storey tower located in Taipei, Taiwan. Open to the public was this building's dampener chamber. Towers this high are subject to heavy wind loads as well as shaking by earthquakes. Subsequently they are designed to move *metres* horizontally, referred to more commonly as lateral directions. Even though design allowances can be made to safely accommodate this kind of movement, occupants subject to this movement can experience motion sickness similar to being on a bobbing boat sailing a choppy ocean. To counteract this, high rise towers are equipped with a large mass dampener. To see one such dampener with my own eyes made me appreciate what an engineering marvel it was. More than three-storeys high, a 600-tonne steel ball is suspended in mid-air in the middle of the tower's floorplate. As the tower experiences any sort of load causing it to move, the ball counteracts the movement; absorbing it and moving instead of the building.

Not that Mascot Towers ever needed a 600-tonne tuned mass dampener, it's clear that it did not benefit from any competent engineering forethought at all during design or construction. Transfer beams suddenly found themselves subject to more load

Chapter 7: Movement

than they were designed for, subsequently placing stress on connected components, thus compromising them. When buildings fall down because of this domino effect, it's called progressive collapse. Prevention of these catastrophes really do start at the beginning; practice safe design, use a concept.

The cracks at Mascot Towers clearly gave cause for alarm. Frustratingly, it appears that they were significant enough to be brought to the attention of the building managers just three years after construction. Well before any construction activity occurred next door, well within any typical warranty period, and *eight* years before the evacuation. Even though the managers did the right thing by appointing a consultant to investigate, the investigation clearly fell short. That's not a criticism of the investigating consultant, because it's entirely possible that the managers didn't want to spend any more money by expanding the consultant's scope to include intrusive investigations. Opening up a building is costly and disruptive, and there's always that fear of the unknown. When you open up, who knows what cost escalation skeletons you'll find. Suddenly time is "at large"; that is, works and costs project uncontrollably into the future with no knowable end date in sight. Sadly, we've watched the possible consequence of this inaction unfold.

We have our observations, now let's consider our deductions. Even the local MP, Ron Hoening, went on record during a TV interview with an impulsive, perhaps emotionally driven, deduction of his own, "[The neighbouring building] is completed but it has not yet even been occupied and then all of a sudden, cracks start developing in the basement of this building …it's just suspicious when you get that cracking."[4]

Suspicious indeed but not tested. Simplifying this deduction goes a little like this: A tower next door is constructed, which involves vibrating plant and equipment, and around the same time cracks appear in our building. I deduce that the vibrating plant and equipment resulted in cracking to our building. It's not difficult to eliminate this deduction, since there's a record of cracks appearing well before construction activity ever took place next door, *and* the neighbouring developer protected themselves by recording the condition of surrounding areas before they got to work. That condition report shows the cracks to Mascot Towers! This is surely enough to bring this deduction under intense scrutiny. To eliminate it completely one would run each of these lines of inquiry to ground by understanding fully the detail of the observed cracks at year three and if they were the same locations as those observed when residents had to evacuate. The same goes for the condition report produced by next door. Yet, when the neighbouring developer was sued for the allegation this deduction is based on, they agreed to an out of court settlement. Moving on.

On 25 June 2019 NSW Deputy Premier, John Barilaro publicly declared a theory of his own, that Mascot Towers was sinking due to a drop in the water table (presumably based on reports he had read),[5] once more attributing this drop to the neighbouring construction work. The sinking the Deputy Premier likely referred to is known as differential settlement. This is where different parts of a building sink at different rates, causing tension to various building elements, eventually compromising the structure allowing part of it to move downward with the moving ground.

So far, we have two deductions readily offered by public servants who have no qualms putting on building detective hats of their own. I can offer three more making a total of five hypothesis with the potential to explain our mystery of what caused Mascot Towers to move so much:

- Vibration of plant and equipment from an adjacent construction site cause the building to crack in various areas;

- The construction activity from the adjacent site affected the surrounding water table, causing the building to experience differential settlement;

Chapter 7: Movement

- Mascot Towers is built above an underground train station. It's possible that vibrations from transiting trains caused cracks to develop over time, eventually leading to a failure;

- Overall poor workmanship by the builder throughout the property's construction; and

- The inadequately designed structure neglected to consider the full extent of the site context and geological conditions.

Then incumbent NSW Building Commissioner, David Chandler OAM, told a Parliamentary inquiry that the engineering design of the Mascot Towers was "poor" and that "the builder didn't know how to read any construction plans".[6] As always, the conclusion could feature a combination of more than one deduction, and still deductions we have yet to dream up, or reveal themselves during our investigation. All anyone can do is begin the process of eliminating each of these one at a time until we arrive at the deduction that is the most difficult to disprove. That *might* be our conclusion. Only when you can prove it using evidence can it be considered absolutely conclusive.

Detectives have a heavy reliance on people, their perspectives, and insights without which would leave one only seeing part of the picture. The Australian Lutheran World Service (ALWS) is the overseas aid and resettlement agency of the Lutheran Church of Australia. One of their objectives is to protect and uphold the dignity of people, especially children and the vulnerable, to lead lives in peace and safety.[7] To that end, they had operational responsibility of two hospitals in Papua New Guinea and needed help communicating the maintenance needs for each building as part of a grant application to the Australian government.

Travel advice for those travelling in Papua New Guinea did not mince words: exercise a high degree of caution in Papua New Guinea overall due to high levels of serious crime.[8] I'd made a base using a hotel in Madang and had been appointed a security detail.

The Building Detective

On approach to the hotel, it was hard to miss the high perimeter wall topped with razor wire. I pulled out my phone to take a photo, and just as I did two young men at the side of the road entered the frame, gave great smiles and waved. The hospitals' locations presented their own challenges, the second of the two being on a semi-active volcanic island. The first hospital was about a half-hour outside Madang. Our security escort drove us down the highway for a short while before turning off onto a track, which quickly became dense rainforest. After a twenty-minute ascent, driving past people traversing the same route on foot alone, we arrived. It was clear right away this was not like any inspection I had undertaken before.

I learned from the staff and the information they had to hand that the hospital was constructed by volunteers around 1948, using buildings and materials left over from World War II. As I inspected, I walked past babies born only moments earlier, in a structure that was not weathertight or even clean to the standard of my own home, let alone those required for the hygiene of a hospital. It didn't matter: these buildings served a critical function for the local community, without which there would be devastating hardship. A far cry from the client's objective to uphold dignity, especially for children.

Karkar Island is located 64 km north of Madang. Karkar's volcano is part of a chain of fifteen volcanic islands in the western part of the volcanic arc in the Bismarck Sea. It's last recorded eruption was in 2014. Initially, we had chartered a dive boat for the two-hour sail there. However, an up-to-date weather report indicated that there would be rough conditions, so we enacted plan B – a helicopter. I'd been on a helicopter before as a tourist, though it did feel different boarding one for work – a different kind of excitement, maybe. The weather had deteriorated, so the pilot had to fly low along the coast for as long as he could before crossing to the island by the shortest distance, to minimise the time spent over the ocean.

On our approach, the volcano's peak was shrouded by raincloud and all I could see of the hospital was a white dot just off the beach, nestled among green palms. As we got closer, I could see a clear

Chapter 7: Movement

paddock in the middle of the site, presumably for helicopters to land. As we got lower, people looked up, running and lining the perimeter fence. The rotors were still whirring loudly as we stepped out, and a doctor emerged through the fence to greet me and ask what I wanted to do first. The previous plan to sail over gave an allowance of a whole day for inspections. With the helicopter taxi this no longer the case. The pilot reminded me that a storm was coming in and if we wanted to fly back without any problems, the inspection of all hospital buildings had best be completed inside the next couple of hours.

I interviewed the doctor alongside a few others familiar with the site, recording our conversations on my phone with their permission. I reeled off standard requests, asking for information about site problems, keeping it strictly to physical condition each time the doctor veered into operational issues. I made note of water leaks, wall cracks, general damage and so on. I asked him to show me these issues, following which I began the usual methodical approach to ensure that I'd viewed each part of the site as I walked through it.

As it started to rain lightly, my data collection become more frantic. My camera was continually snapping all building surfaces, first getting wide, contextual shots, then identifying defects to be photographed in more detail later. My site contact walked and talked. With my camera in one hand, my other was operating the recorder app on my phone while I dictated my observations and listened to the wealth of information the doctor had to offer. A wall in what used to be a ward had apparently been critically damaged by tremors from the volcano. These weren't cracks you would measure; large openings were evident to many of the structures, and a future tremor would surely destroy them.

Volcanic-tectonic earthquakes (VTs) are caused by slip on a fault near a volcano. Volcanoes are often found in areas of crustal weakness and the mass of the volcano itself adds to the regional strain. Most VT earthquakes have nothing to do with the magmatic system of the volcano but occur in response to regional strain exerted in an area of weak faults. VTs can also be generated from changes of pressure under the volcano caused by the injection or removal of molten rock (magma) from the volcanic system. After the withdrawal of magma from a system, an empty space is left to be filled. The result is a collapse of surrounding rock to fill the void, also creating earthquakes. VT earthquakes can result in land deformation, collapse and/or ground failure but they are usually small and leave no trace on the surface. Under ordinary circumstances, where the structures of today are designed and built against the rigour of building code which makes allowances for seismic risk, these earthquakes usually don't cause damage due to their small size which produces weak shaking. However, these are structures built by volunteers in the 1940s on a remote island.

A vibration is an oscillating movement of particles in an elastic medium (e.g., soil or a building) from both sides of an equilibrium position. They can be characterised by the following parameters: the amplitude of the vibration and the frequency. The amplitude of the vibration is generally characterised by either the displacement, the velocity (generally noted in mm/s) or the acceleration of the oscillatory movement of an object, while the frequency (generally given in Hz) is a function of the return time of one cycle of displacement. Vibrations that are more largely spaced apart in time will have low frequencies and it is generally these vibrations that present a higher risk of damage to buildings.

Two factors directly influence the impacts of vibrations on a building. These are the duration of exposure to a vibration, as well as the distance between the source of vibration and the building or structure. Given this, the extent of damage due to vibrations increases with prolonged exposure, as well as with a reduction of distance between the vibration source and the building.

Under the correct conditions, vibrations generated by an earthquake or construction work can damage a building by two separate mechanisms. The first, by transmitting vibrations directly to the building structure through the support points (seating) of the foundations. And second, by causing displacement of the soils beneath the foundation, resulting in a loss of support to the foundation and settlement. In either case, the damage observed is usually greater in the area of a building located nearest to the vibration source (such as within the basement or on the foundations), especially when the vibration source and the building are in close proximity to each other. As well, the first signs of damage, generally aesthetic in nature, will be observed in "fragile" locations prone to damage, in particular at the junction of walls and ceilings, or at the corners of door and window openings. Old interior plaster finishes are more brittle and sensitive to vibrations than the common drywall panels currently used in building construction.

When significant vibrations affect a building, structural damage such as cracking of foundation walls or cracking in masonry elements, as well as excessive sloping of floors, can be observed. This damage appears similarly with other structural issues that may affect a building. This makes it necessary to obtain all the data and information concerning the source of vibrations to properly establish the exact cause of the damage.

With all this in mind, when available, the nature of the construction work, its location, the type of machinery used, and the duration of machinery use provide important information for our investigation. In addition, pre-construction survey reports sometimes make it possible to identify damage that was already present before the work began. Finally, the monitoring of vibrations on site during construction makes it possible to certify that contractors have complied with local regulations (if applicable), or generally accepted practices. For example, the City of Toronto Municipal Code establishes limits regarding the maximum vibration peak velocity during construction work,[9] as do many other cities. It's still possible, in the case of historic and heritage buildings, that limits lower than those specified in the local regulations are established in order to preserve the integrity of heritage buildings since they are generally less tolerant to vibration-related movements.

No one talks about earthquakes in Australia, let alone the loss of life they have caused. On average 100 earthquakes of magnitude 3 or more are recorded in Australia each year. Earthquakes above magnitude 5.0 occur on average every one-to-two years and magnitude 6.0 every 10 years.[10] You'd be forgiven for wondering how this is possible since there are no major fault lines located on the Australasian land mass; the country lies in the middle of the Australian tectonic plate. This is known as an intraplate setting. Parts of Australia experience intraplate earthquakes as opposed to interplate earthquakes which occur at the edge of a tectonic plate. The Australian plate is the fastest moving continental land mass on Earth and is colliding into the fastest moving tectonic plate, the Pacific plate to Australia's north east. These combined movements cause a build-up of stress in the interior of the Australian plate, which then releases during intraplate quakes, such as the magnitude 6.7 earthquake in Meckering, Western Australia, 1986. Meckering was so close to the epicentre, given the small size of the town the majority of the buildings suffered significant failures. When inspecting Meckering Primary School, it was great to see that some buildings were preserved, including a timber constructed church relocated to the school grounds for use as a kindergarten. Since the reason I was there was to record defects that impact the ability for the school to safely conduct its operations, I had to ensure adequate context was required for the timber building; rectification of the misaligned timber floors (revealing air gaps to outside) may not be appropriate. What might be more appropriate is to consider how feasible it is to change the building's use and therefore reduce its overall risk profile. The '80s saw another high magnitude quake in Australia, this time on the opposite coast. A 5.7 earthquake in Newcastle, New South Wales, which destroyed one building constructed from unreinforced brick masonry. On its southern coast in Victora (VIC), on 28 May 2023 at a depth of 3km, 20,000 people felt tremors, the largest in a century in VIC.[11]

Chapter 7: Movement

Straddling the boundary of the Australian and Pacific plates, New Zealand is no stranger to the destructive power of tectonic forces. The Christchurch earthquake of February 2011, a magnitude 6.3 quake, served as a grim reminder of the region's seismic volatility. The quake struck the Canterbury region, its epicentre a mere 6.7 kilometres southeast of Christchurch's city centre, causing widespread devastation and claiming 185 lives in New Zealand's fifth-deadliest disaster.[12]

In the aftermath, the nation embarked on a mission to fortify its structures against future quakes. As the dust settled in Christchurch, the focus shifted to assessing and repairing the damage. Engineers, mostly involved in residential and some commercial assessments for insurance companies, adhered to new guidelines issued by the Ministry of Business, Innovation, and Employment. These guidelines outlined performance requirements for damaged buildings to ensure consistent assessments across the board. A significant aspect of the post-earthquake response was the categorisation of Christchurch land into distinct technical categories. Category 1 denoted stable land, Category 2 included somewhat loose but not waterlogged soil, and Category 3 encompassed fairly waterlogged areas that could still support construction. The infamous red zones, however, were deemed unfit for building due to severe liquefaction damage. Liquefaction is a phenomenon where shaking forces water to the surface, causing the ground to move like quicksand. Before the quake, Christchurch was believed to be less susceptible to liquefaction due to its proximity to the fault line, leading to an inadequate level of preparedness. The role of the geotechnical report became paramount in any investigation. It provided insights into the ground conditions and informed appropriate repair methodologies. Christchurch's construction featured a mix of raft foundations and low-set timber pile foundations, the latter unaffected by termites absent in New Zealand, but vulnerable to marine borers. The collapse of the Pyne Gould building, a seven-storey reinforced concrete structure built in the 1960s, highlighted the dangers of outdated designs. The under-reinforced main core wall failed completely, indicating multiple oversights during the design phase. In response, New Zealand implemented new building standards, requiring upgrades for older buildings. However, these upgrades varied based on the building's importance. Residential buildings needed to meet only 34% of the new standard,[13] determined by identifying the weakest failure point. More critical structures, like hospitals, required more comprehensive upgrades, sometimes involving animated models for dynamic analysis.

The human element of this tragedy was most evident in the residential sector. Homeowners, faced with the prospect of losing their compromised homes, often resisted demolition. Conversely, others exaggerated minor damages, hoping to have their buildings written off. Central Christchurch, once a bustling area, transformed into a ghost town dotted with empty plots. Despite some new developments, much of the area remains a large construction site, a stark reminder of the earthquake's enduring impact.

In wrapping up this chapter on movement in buildings, it's only fair to make a special mention for the identification of movement types and causes exhibited by cracks to masonry brick and blockwork. Interpreting cracks is an art in itself. Deductions can be made simply by understanding crack width, direction and context. In fact, there are whole books written on the subject to assist practitioners to develop their interpretation craft. The *Practical Guide to Diagnosing Structural Movement In Buildings*[14] by Malcolm Holland MRICS is an excellent resource, outlining first principals with clarity ahead of demonstrating how to apply them using a variety of examples. Malcolm suggests a user of his guide would be able to diagnose the majority of cracks within just a few minutes. CSIRO also provides a white paper written for homeowners that provides a good, basic grounding in building movement and cracking.[15]

Chapter 8: Water

> *"Empty your mind, be formless. Shapeless, like water. If you put water into a cup, it becomes the cup. You put water into a bottle and it becomes the bottle. You put it in a teapot, it becomes the teapot. Now, water can flow or it can crash.*
>
> *Be water, my friend."*

Bruce Lee

After 1am in Surfside, a suburb just north of Miami in Florida, people stopped as they walked past an apartment building to use their phones to record a stream of water they noticed discharging into the basement like a small waterfall. In the United States, apartment blocks are referred to as condominiums, or condos for short. If you've ever wondered why, it's from Latin, con- 'together with' + dominium 'right of ownership'. Meanwhile inside the condo, residents on the upper levels heard loud noises and saw cracks suddenly appear. Little did they know that the first-storey car park had already partially collapsed. Around seven minutes later the tower sustained a partial progressive collapse. On 24 June 2021, 55 of the 136 apartment units across its 12-storey height, fell to the ground killing 98 people.[1]

In this case study, we're not going to speculate the decisions that may have taken place throughout the tower's lifecycle for the purposes of determining the causal chain leading to the collapse, which arguably goes all the way back to the design phase. At least one of the concrete floor slabs was designed as "too level". As in, it wasn't sloped enough for water to fall off of it; slopes or angles for this purpose are called 'falls'. This detail is important, because we're going to focus on the implications of standing water on a concrete surface and why this can create the physical conditions necessary to propagate a failure like the one Champlain Tower South succumbed to.

A building's life is often referred to as its lifecycle, broadly phased as follows: design, construction, operation, decommissioning. One can expect the lifecycle of a building constructed today to last up to 60 years. When it collapsed, Champlain Tower South was fast approaching its 40th year and in Miami-Dade County 40-year recertifications apply to buildings with more than ten occupants or with a total floor area greater than $185m^2$.[2] This recertification can take up to a year to complete. It ensures a building continues to meet relevant requirements to continue to be safely used.

The 1970s project was the first new construction in Surfside following a moratorium on new development imposed by Miami-Dade County due to water and sewer infrastructure problems in Surfside. In 1979, developers paid the city $200,000 USD (equivalent to $870,000 USD in 2025) to fund the replacement of the sewer system and secure approval for the construction of the condos.[3]

A 2018 inspection performed by the engineering firm Morabito Consultants identified a "major error" in the construction of the pool deck,[4] where the waterproofing layer was not sloped. Rainwater collected on the waterproofing layer remained until it could evaporate. Over the years, the concrete slabs below the pool deck had been damaged by this water. The report noted the waterproofing below the pool deck was beyond its useful life and needed to be completely removed and replaced. The firm wrote that "failure to replace waterproofing in the near future will cause the extent of the concrete deterioration to expand exponentially," and that the repair

Chapter 8: Water

would be "extremely expensive." The ceiling slabs of the parking garage, which sat below the pool deck, exhibited several cracks and cases of exposed reinforcing bar or rebar from spalling. In October 2020, initial repairs around the pool could not be completed because (according to engineers) the deterioration had penetrated so deeply that repairs would have risked destabilising that area.

On 9 April 2021, a letter to residents had outlined a $15 million USD remedial-works program, noting that concrete deterioration was accelerating and had become "much worse" since the 2018 report.[5] Although the roof repairs pursuant to the consultant's report were underway at the time of the collapse, remedial concrete works had not yet begun. In addition to the freshwater infiltrations from the potentially defectively constructed pool deck, a maintenance manager had reported ingress of salt water, which can cause more aggressive spalling. Salt water is a much better electrolyte than fresh water because of the dissolved salts. This higher conductivity accelerates the electrochemical reactions that lead to corrosion.

The National Institute of Standards and Technology (NIST) is an agency of the United States Department of Commerce, tasked with promoting American innovation and industrial competitiveness. NIST's activities are organised into physical science laboratory programs that include nanoscale science and technology, engineering, information technology, neutron research, material measurement, and physical measurement. They are currently amid investigating all matters in connection with the collapse of Champlain Tower South. NIST investigations are thorough and typically take years to complete. Their report on the collapsed World Trade Centre took four years to complete. A contributing factor under investigation is long-term degradation of reinforced concrete structural support in the basement-level parking garage under the pool deck, due to water penetration and corrosion of the reinforcing steel.

The team's preliminary evaluation of physical and historical evidence revealed how the construction of the pool deck deviated from design requirements. In May 2023, a portion of the evidence was moved into a second warehouse that provided enough space to safely access the specimens. The NIST investigation team extracted more than 300 concrete cores and rebar samples for materials testing.[6] So far, the average tested concrete strength for various types of structural elements such as slabs and columns *exceed* the specified design strength for those elements. The team will continue to conduct strength tests and detailed statistical analysis before drawing general conclusions. The NIST team sought as many observations as possible to contribute to their investigation, including actively seeking additional photos or videos of the building during the collapse, inviting the public to submit them online through the NIST Disaster Data Portal.

Distinct from possible construction defects, an analysis of European Remote-Sensing Satellite data by Florida International University indicates that the building had been sinking during the 1990s at a significant rate of about two millimetres per year. While 97% of Miami Beach had been stable, 1,555 of 18,949 points in Miami Beach had been sinking, at a rate of less than one millimetre per year.[7] A building collapse due to sinking is likely only if parts are sinking at different rates, creating tensions that weaken the structure; this is the differential settlement we know from the Mascot Towers case study. The researchers noted that other overbuilt areas were sinking at a significantly faster rate, such as on the artificial islands in Biscayne Bay – up to 3.8 millimetre per year. All of this speculation as to a potential contributing cause for the collapse was eliminated by NIST. Among a number of items being investigated, one of NIST's hypothesis was subsidence or excessive settling, which they eliminated by studying subsurface conditions to confirm any evidence of sinkholes, of which there were none that indicated enough to be a contributing cause.

Chapter 8: Water

NIST's draft report with findings and recommendations is projected to be ready for public review in 2026. It's likely they will determine several factors happened simultaneously to cause the collapse. Champlain Towers South Condominium Association had just $777,000 USD in their reserve fund to cover $16.2 million USD of repairs that were neglected for reasons yet to be determined. The cost in the end was $1.02 billion USD and 98 lives. Condominium associations, or homeowner associations (HOA) have a reputation for being overly democratic, with an expertise barrier that is too low, and ultimately do not contain competent advisors. This is not unique to the USA, I've seen the same ring true of their Australian counterparts, body corporate committees.

****

I had a very personal experience related to a water problem in my own home, which I offer as a case study displaying ODEC in action from start to finish. Having a personal stake in the problem inevitably introduced an emotional element, demonstrating the impact it had on the ebb and flow of the investigation.

One commonly commissioned report from a building consultant is a pre-purchase report. This report can go by a few names: pre-acquisition report, technical due diligence report, a pre-purchase residential inspection, or a homebuyer's report. A residential homebuyer may make an offer to buy a property subject to terms which may include obtaining a pre-purchase report. The homebuyer then has a limited period of time to appoint a building consultant, arrange the inspection, obtain their report, and understand how its findings impact the transaction. Anything material discovered by the inspection that was not otherwise disclosed by the vendor during the sale process may very well become the means upon which the house price is negotiated down. The same process occurs for multi-million-dollar commercial transactions. I've seen a price chip of millions from the asking price because we found the lift banks were more than thirty years old, parts were no longer available and they were due for replacement. I've seen a buyer walk away from a shopping centre because they couldn't get comfort on how a dry cleaner disposing its chemical waste may have impacted the indoor air quality of the centre. It's no different when it comes to a discerning and diligent buyer of a home.

Say the underlying timbers making up the roof frame are compromised, and the roof requires replacement in the next twelve months, less the risk the next storm season tearing the roof off the house. Let's also say the roof size reflects a replacement price tag of $20,000. The now informed buyer becomes empowered to either walk away from the purchase or revise their offer down by $20,000. The relatively small price they paid for their report will have allowed them to keep $20,000 back to plan their roof replacement, which would have otherwise been pocketed by the vendor.

I bought my first house in 2022. Approaching my forties you might argue I climbed onto that ladder later than some. My wife and I had moved countries, already married and had children, then a pandemic happened. Ultimately, everyone's circumstances are different and there is no right time to buy. As the metaphor about investing goes: the best time to plant a tree is yesterday, the second-best time is today. Although, we risk getting more philosophical when we argue whether or not the home you live in, and have no plans to move away from, is an investment or not. Moving on.

Speculating my own first purchase at this point of my career, I felt like I was prepared for anything. We researched the areas where we wanted to live, which included things like schools, public transport links, and amenity. Amenity was anything useful or recreational that was within walking distance or a short drive. Things like local shops, good coffee, play parks, water, bushwalks, etc. When we inspected open homes, I focused my detective's eye. I'd try to ignore any emotions I was having and look for clues to issues. Most of the time things would jump out: evidence of termite activity that the vendor thought they'd concealed well enough, or timber decay to the bottoms of supporting columns resting on galvanised stirrups. The stirrups did a good job of hiding most of the decay, and often

Chapter 8: Water

enough the perspective of people walking through a home would not change from their own eye level. In the case of the decayed columns, what the rest of the house had to offer for the price, for me, was not outweighed by having to deal with the replacement of a verandah.

After some time in the market, we had looked at well over forty homes. With two young kids in tow, it was exhausting. The first couple of times the kids tried to turn the TV on, play with toys, and needed to use the toilet. We developed a strategy where one of us would go in whilst the other stayed in the car with the kids. I'd record my walkthrough on my phone and we'd look at it together afterward. Then we stumbled across the home from where I write this now.

The house itself was smaller than what we were looking for, but it was on a big block in a cul-de-sac. Most interestingly, however, was that it had relisted and dropped its price *twice* in the space of a month. My curiosity was piqued. What was going on with this house that it would drop its price twice in four weeks? At the very least it would make inspecting the open home a little more interesting than normal, knowing that something was there to be found, and challenging myself to uncover it.

It was a beautifully dry Queensland spring morning and it hadn't rained for a few weeks. Having a little water in play is normally a good assist, possibly revealing water related issues that would have otherwise remained undiscovered. No matter, perhaps some staining or tide marks to ceilings, walls and carpets would indicate something going on. As I walked through the house, I was oblivious to groups of people wandering around and the agent explaining the potential of the outdoor space. I was on a mission. I slowly walked room by room, methodically scanning all of the surfaces for any indication of something that shouldn't be there, the house was determined to keep its secret. The vendor had taken the time and care to stage the home, hiring furniture, artwork and presenting it to be warm and inviting. A fresh-looking tin of paint found sitting in the shed indicating they'd gone to the effort to repaint the house ready for sale. Why on earth had its price been dropped so dramatically?

To speculate the price drops for a moment, one might deduce as follows: the property was listed on the market and found a preferred offer. Terms were agreed to before going under a conditional contract to buy, which includes "subject to" clauses, making the contract to buy conditional upon specific matters. These commonly include obtaining finance from the bank and obtaining pre-purchase building and pest reports. It's easy to imagine how the buyer's building report confirmed something critical about this property, and that whatever it was, was serious enough for the buyer to revise their offer. Subsequently, the vendor rejected the offer and the sale fell apart. The vendor relisted with a lower price, then it happened again! A new offer, another report, maybe the same issue was uncovered, maybe it was a different issue entirely, resulting in another revised offer, and the vendor rejecting it once again.

Could it be connected to the straight hairline crack to the ceiling following the length of the lounge? Remember from the last chapter, such hairline cracks are generally not a cause for concern. They are, more often than not, associated with shrinkage of plasterwork or paint (remember the paint tin in the shed?), or undetectable movement that every structure experiences which is why we install things like movement or control joints at fixed intervals. All buildings move. Could the deal killer be connected to a seemingly randomly located drain pipe embedded within the concrete patio? This pipe appeared to be in service of taking water away from a spoon drain at the bottom of a retaining wall, but its location and position looked as though it went under the concrete patio slab and the house ground baring slab. The pipe's installation coming across altogether as the haphazard afterthought of someone taking a stab in the dark. However, there was no evidence of any associated issues within the house. Sure, there was minor issues with the house, but the sum of my findings didn't amount to anything that was

Chapter 8: Water

insurmountable. Surely whatever was going on here, if anyone was going to get on top of it, it might as well be me. A big plot with development potential at a dropped price? A corner nook in the back garden where I could finally have my pizza oven? It was too late; my emotions were already at work clouding my judgement. This was my entry into the market.

We low balled an offer and figured if we got it, we got it. Terms: Finance pre-approved and …no building report required. *No building report required*? That's right. What was I going to learn from a pre-purchase building report that I didn't already see with my own eyes? Sure, the previous two speculative buyers uncovered something, but what? As far as I can tell, this house has stood for almost forty years and there was no indication it was about to fall down. Anything beyond that I felt was solvable. With house prices everywhere rising, it felt like a measured risk.

The vendor couldn't accept our offer quick enough.

A short thirty days later settlement was reached and the house was ours. Two days after that, I threw my hose down each of the stormwater drain pipes to ascertain their condition for myself. The house sits upon a sloped site, so the setup of the drainage and the spoon drain to the back and the sides of the house is designed to redirect overland stormwater flow around the house and down to the road. Each of the two stormwater drains flowing down the boundaries revealed blockages in the below ground pipe, as well as likely breakages, evident from the dying, waterlogged grass above specific sections. Not great but fixable at low cost and some effort. I threw my hose nozzle into the drain pipe located to the middle rear of the house …and nothing happened. Not at first anyway. No water was discharging from any of the kerb adapters on the road. The water didn't appear to be coming out anywhere. It wasn't even backing up, suggesting it wasn't blocked. Where was this water going? A couple of hours later, dampness manifested to the carpet in my boys' bedroom located roughly in the middle of the house. To adapt a quote from Mike Tyson: if you're not humble, then life will visit humbleness upon you.[8]

Ruled by my emotions more than a rational enquiring mind, the reason for the dampness was obvious: this aggregate pipe goes under the house and must be broken in the middle. Each time it takes in water, it leaks, and through capillary action the water moves through the ground and the slab and appears as a damp patch on my boys' carpet. It rained that weekend. The spoon drain filled up, the drain took in water, and the carpet got wet again. Now I was certain and I capped the end of the pipe to prevent any water from entering.

The carpet dried out and stayed dry. For a few days at least. Turns out all I had done was rule out an initial hypothesis. Over the preceding months, I began to rule out what wasn't causing this issue. The kitchen is adjacent to the bedroom where the damp patch appeared. Looking upon the kitchen, the taps and sink are against the outside wall. However, our fridge was against the internal wall closest to the offending area. I pulled the fridge and floor unit away to inspect. It was dry. After everyone went to bed and I was confident that none of the taps or toilet were going to be used overnight, I made a note of the reading on the water meter. In the morning before anyone was up, I checked the reading against what I wrote down... it had moved. Something was going on, there was a leak somewhere.

I climbed into the roof void and inspected the roof tiles, timber trusses and insulation for any evidence of repeated wetting or deterioration. Everything was in a good condition. Inspecting directly above where the damp carpet was, the void of the stud wall was concealed by a timber baton – a top plate, restricting me from looking directly down inside the wall.

The house was designed so that all incoming water and outgoing waste water was located to the back wall of the house, making it straight forward for the incoming line to continue along the soffit, with a junction down to each service: the bathroom, the kitchen and

Chapter 8: Water

the laundry. Nothing indicated any leaks to the hot and cold-water pipes. The waste water pipes however, follow from each room directly into the concrete slab. Could one of these pipes follow under the slab to reach the sewer connection in the road? I took two of the waste water drains out of the equation for three days (kitchen sink and laundry sink). During this period, it had not rained for a couple of weeks. The damp patch reappeared on the bedroom carpet.

Working from home one day, my wife and kids were at work and school. The house fell short of silence. Interrupting my tinnitus was another, faint, dull hiss. I could hear something that should not be. I followed it to the toilet's cistern. Being an older cistern, it had seen better days, and it's ballcock and valve were apparently not fully closing after the cistern filled back up with water. This meant that water continued to be slowly added to the cistern, simply overflowing into its waste pipe. I jiggled the valve and it closed. The water flow stopped as well as the hissing sound. That night I checked the water meter, then again in the morning. A problem I didn't know I had, was solved. This ruled out leaking mains water pipes from my main problem. I had drawn a correlation between the water main and the damp patch, but correlation does not mean causation.

By this point, especially with a few weeks of a dry spell under our belt, the waste water drain from the bathroom was the last variable in play. The dampness manifested cyclically: it would dry out then become damp again, most days, suggesting that it coincides with discharging the bath and shower waste water. It became the primary hypothesis and therefore had to be tested. It also meant for the hypothesis to be true, that there must be a break in the waste water pipe close to where the damp was manifesting. Now we must ask: how could a break occur to an assumed 100 millimetre PVC waste water pipe located below a ground baring concrete slab?

At this point, it's worth explaining the history of the spoon drain at the rear of the house. In Australia, there are a couple of real estate rent and buy websites that are prevalent in everyone's search for a home. Listings remain on the websites after the sale, simply noted as "off the market". Often times, the photography from older listings can be found.

My house was last listed in 2008 when the original 1985 owner put it up for sale. Astonishingly, the images are preserved for anyone to look at. It was here that I made the discovery the spoon drain used to be screeded with stones, presenting as a sort of edging feature along the bottom of the retaining wall. A spoon drain's primary job is to collect any seepage water from a retaining wall and carry it away, you can often find them along the walls of basement car parks.

Before I capped the pipe, I tried to throw a CCTV camera down it to see what I could, only to be met with stones; it was full of them. My hand could reach inside to grab some but the awkward angle limited my reach. The stones I pulled out were those from the 2008 listing photographs. As it turned out, the owner before me didn't just get rid of these stones: they were all in the garden bed held by the retaining wall. Why?

With the mystery pipe in mind, was it a coincidence that the carpet got wet when it took in water, or is it part of the equation? After all, it must go somewhere. What if the previous owner thought they were being clever by connecting this storm water drain pipe into the waste water pipe? Illegal yes, but still possible. Penetrating the waste water pipe to make this connection, exacerbated by stones inside the pipe, could explain how the waste water pipe could be broken.

I admit on reflection, this hypothesis is harebrained, but a working hypothesis, nonetheless. So long as we have a hypothesis in play, we can work to rule it out, as well as leaving open the opportunity to learn and discover new data as we do. I made some enquiries and contacted a recommended local plumber. I can quite imagine how one must feel having such an issue, with no idea why it's happening,

Chapter 8: Water

and simply trusting a plumber to spend the time to figure it out. It's not possible to estimate how many hours are required to do so, and unless you have a bottomless pit of money, the fear is real; how much is this going to cost? And not even to fix the problem, this is just to figure out what the problem is, so then it can then be fixed, again at further cost.

My instructions to the plumber were clear: I needed them to send their CCTV drain camera (which was a lot better than the one I had access to) down the wastewater pipe, to ascertain its direction, distance, and condition. This made their time at my house finite, subject to a call out fee, and then an hourly rate after that. This exercise shouldn't take more than an hour at which point I can regroup and determine next steps. It's worth pointing out that this highlights the value of a building consultant. Clients sometimes ask why they should consult with me first rather than go straight to a registered structural engineer. The answer is simple: if you don't yet fully understand the nature of the problem you have, you risk spending more money on an intrusive structural engineer's investigation that you *might not even need*. If it turns out you do need a structural engineer, it is your building consultant's, quicker, holistic and unintrusive process that produced the necessary hypothesis for the structural engineer to prove or disprove in a highly targeted way.

So back to my house. The plumber's scope would hopefully confirm or rule out my hypothesis: that the waste pipe went under the house, that it was broken, and that I could ask the plumber for a quote to undertake a sleeve repair. A no-dig repair method where a new intact pipe is pushed into a broken host pipe and is expanded to seal off breaks. A technical and pricey rectification, but one that's less intrusive and still less expensive than excavating the slab of my house.

Not only did the plumber deploy their camera, based on my descriptions he brought a colleague and a below ground locator. Good plumber. The camera entered the toilet stack at the back of the house (the larger pipe that your toilet discharges into, also has pipe that continues up to the roof that vents smell: a soil vent stack or pipe) and instantly we could see on the monitor what the wide angle lens could see, and a heads up display that included how many metres along the pipe we had travelled. "Ok mate, ninety degrees left, two metres in."

Observing with bated breath, had I seen that right? "The pipe follows *away* from the house?" I ask. The camera at the end of the snake like cable has a device on it called a *Sonde*, which emits a signal. This signal is picked up by Old Mate's radar wand, a brand called *Rigid*, as he continued to float above it, walking along the patio slab with it as his colleague continued to feed the snake down the pipe. "Yeah mate, looks like every waste water pipe comes away from the back of your house and connects in along this pipe. Go turn the kitchen tap on, will ya?"

Sure enough, the monitor displayed each junction, and here was the junction for the kitchen sink, water clearly trickling in. We continued on: the line followed parallel to the back of the house, and made a 90-degree left turn down the driveway. To my amazement, the cable on the reel had more than enough left to travel the twenty odd metres down the driveway to reveal the connection with the sewer in the road, Old Mate's Rigid wand tracking its location all of the way. All of the below ground pipe work was in great condition with no dents or breaks.

And none of the waste water pipes went under the house.

"Hey before you leave, can you check out this drain pipe here?"

Since I knew it was full of stones, it was a long shot, but it was a chance to see if there was any way to see anything I couldn't before. I'm not a plumber, and it is likely that plumbers who face various problems like this day in and day out, think in a different way than I do. Anyone that does a different job to you, will likely think in a different way than you do, and that is valuable.

Chapter 8: Water

The key difference between the camera I used, and the one they used, was the end had these big ribs on it that extend away from the lens. Whilst mine without ribs simply scrapped gunk from the inside of the pipe and covered the lens, theirs kept the lens clear from the edge of the pipe, stopping any gunk being collected covering up the lens. The ribs were so big that it wasn't going to get past these stones. "Hold on mate, let me switch this out."

Handily, he switched the large ribs out for a much smaller version. With a little force, he pushed past the stones. We were off to the races. Old Mate had his locating wand at the ready. The pipe took an immediate left turn. It followed down the patio, parallel to the retaining wall and stopped eight metres along. It didn't go anywhere near the house. I'd now run out of hypothesis. I'd finally arrived at the point I'd been avoiding for so long: opening up. The intrusive investigation they avoided at Mascot Towers. It evoked all those feelings associated with escalation: increased costs and a likely disruption to my household's operations. General uncertainty on how long the investigation, disruption and costs can go on for.

This can still be controlled. Opening up is targeted, measured, and thoughtful. In my case, it was time to lift the affected carpet away from its grippers to reveal the concrete slab below in order to confirm if the concrete slab is cracked or broken in any way, and generally to gather any other data that may be yielded during the process. My mind was racing out of control, doomsdaying all sorts of possibilities. Was there a sinkhole full of groundwater under my house? Was it was washing away the strata the ground slab bears upon? Was a section of my house going to collapse in the night whilst my children slept?

Let's regroup. We have a damp patch cyclically appearing and drying out, located at ground slab level, directly under a timber framed, internal stud wall. Each time it happens, the carpet adjacent to the internal wall becomes damp too. This is not magic, witchcraft or sorcery. This is water and it comes from three possible sources:

Stormwater:

- Roof is leaking: rain water gets in between roof tiles, and drips onto the top of the timber stud partition between the bedroom and the kitchen and releases at slab level, under the skirting to the carpet.
- Perforated or broken pipe carries stormwater from spoon drain under the house slab, and water moves through a path of least resistance in the slab.

Town water:

- Waste water pipes from kitchen and laundry travel under the house slab.
- Waste water pipe from bathroom overflow relief gully travels under the house slab.
- The back of the fridge is leaking. Although not plumbed in, frost free fridges use a drain pan. This pan collects condensation, in normal operation evaporates, but when faulty, may overflow.
- There's a leak beneath the kitchen sink (potentially under the kickboard) which slowly travels beneath the kitchen floor tiles to its easiest point of relief.

That leaves the third possible water source, and one that strikes fear into the heart of any unsuspecting homeowner: groundwater.

Groundwater is found in aquifers which are below ground, geological formations able to store and transmit water. The geology of Australia is diverse, therefore the types of aquifers vary. Most of Australia's built environment is atop an aquifer. In Perth, Western Australia, groundwater is used in community parks and recreation areas, school grounds, local businesses and 1 in 4 household gardens through the installation of groundwater bore pumps.[9] These devices take advantage of groundwater as a water supply, by using a motor to pump water up a pipe, penetrating metres from underground. Many areas, especially those that are remote, rely on

Chapter 8: Water

groundwater. It is the reason that a characteristic brown and orange stain is prevalent throughout Western Australia, from Perth to the bush. It can be seen on pavement surfaces, signpost poles, garden walls and house gables. As water is brought up to the surface, iron bacteria comes with it. When iron bacteria mixes with oxygen it changes colour to brown. Newer bore systems will filter iron to mitigate these stains and acid cleaning can remove the stains (I have a theory that this is why WA's sign posts and traffic light poles are yellow, whilst the other states aren't – to blend in with the stains. Please contact me if you can confirm this).

The type of aquifer my house sits atop of in south east Queensland is an alluvial aquifer. This is formed of sediments such as gravel, sand and silt deposited by nearby creeks, and typically saturated with water. The position or level of the top of the saturated water is the water table. This position may change due to seasonal rain changes and changes in groundwater consumption. The theory that the cyclically damp patch in the carpet was caused by groundwater is a long shot, but it may hold up. There was a period on the run up to the summer (also known as the wet season in Queensland) where the damp patch didn't appear at all. This could be tested by playing a waiting game; monitoring what happens as summer eases off, moving into autumn and winter.

With these conditions in mind, we can formulate deductions based on groundwater being a cause:

Groundwater:

- An artesian well brings groundwater to the surface without pumping because it is under pressure within an aquifer. Eventually passing through a crack or path of least resistance in the ground floor slab of my house.

- The ground profile prevalent to the local area includes compacted clay, upon which foundations and ground baring slabs must be correctly designed for. Seepage water is sitting on top of the compacted clay coming from the slope behind the house, and through piezometric pressure the water comes and goes through a crack or path of least resistance in the slab.

There is one more thing I can do to rule out groundwater before doing anything intrusive. Test the moisture in the carpet for fluoride. If fluoride is present then we can conclude the water is coming from mains town water, if not then it is rain or groundwater.

Things only get more intrusive and destructive from there. For example, drilling a hole wide enough through the slab so that I could insert the CCTV camera and have a look to see what I can find. Maybe a void? Maybe water will spring up through the hole and flood my house? If drilling a hole didn't yield anything, then I'd progress to using a concrete saw to cut a 400x400 millimetre square hole in the slab. One that I could fit my head inside, or the width of a shovel, and that could be rectified with fresh concrete afterwards. This would require using a scanner beforehand, to detect the position of the steel reinforcement and making sure my hole was made between the bars, minimising any damage. I hadn't yet enquired with the local authority if they had any original as-built drawings of my house in their archives. Let's not get carried away just yet.

I haphazardly lifted the corner of the carpet up to reveal the extent of the damage to date: areas of black mould to the underside of the carpet, the underlay, and the timber carpet grippers. That wasn't all; a regiment of ants tracked along all edges, no doubt ecstatic that I'd discovered their warm moist outpost. The concrete was in good condition, with nothing to add beyond the concentric rings of damp staining emanating from the affected area below the stud wall.

The other side of the internal, plasterboard lined, stud wall could be discreetly opened up: There stood my freestanding, temporary, kitchen floor unit, which I was able to move out of the way, and move back again to conceal my poor workmanship, alleviating the concerns of my key stakeholder (my wife). Breaking a hole in a wall

Chapter 8: Water

to have a look at what's going on inside is not a case of bashing away with a hammer and hoping for the best. A stud is a vertical piece of timber that forms part of the frame of the wall, reaching from the bottom plate to the top plate (the part that stopped me looking down into it before). It is what the plasterboard sheets are screwed to. Using a stud finder, a handheld device you slide along a wall which beeps when it detects a stud, I pencilled off two studs which would be the edges of my hole that I'd cut out and drew a line 400 millimetres up from the floor. Cutting this rectangle piece of plasterboard out would offer me a big enough opening for a meaningful inspection, as well as give me the best chance to reinstate the section I removed by screwing it back onto each of the studs, plastering over the damage and repainting.

Using a sharp craft knife, I cut along the pencilled outline of my opening in the wall, repeating the cuts until making it through the plasterboard, minimising any dust. I pried the section off to be greeted by a small huntsman spider, who rightly scurried up the inside of the wall where I couldn't catch it, probably to alert all of the bird sized hunstman spiders that have happily lived there for so long. I could see the concentric rings stains to the inside face of the opposite sheet of plasterboard, indicating where the majority of the dampness was located: ground zero appeared to be directly below the bottom plate of the stud wall, the horizontal piece of timber that interfaces directly with the slab forming the bottom of the wall frame. I wasn't going to see anything else unless I cut a section of the bottom plate out at the apparent centre of the of concentric ring stains.

Suddenly my hand was wet. I lifted it up to find a small puddle of water on the floor. Rather alarmed, my first thought was, "this is happening right now, the water is coming up through the ground!" Looking for the origin of the water I found a very small hole, around 3-4 millimetre, between two of the floor tiles where the tile grout had deteriorated and left an opening right up against the skirting. The water wasn't coming from here though, it was *entering* through here. I followed a small trail of water which tracked along the skirting of the kitchen wall …toward the fridge! Right there and then, the fridge's drain pan chose to overflow. The water came from the fridge's drain pan, tracked along the skirting, entered through a small hole between two tiles, and settled in underneath the stud wall. All along it was a faulty fridge. Were it not for the carpet adjacent the wall on the other side showing up its stains, this little damp event may have gone completely unnoticed until the plasterboard eventually decided to crumble, and small sections of the timber frame had turned to mush.

Naturally I felt rather silly as I had confidently ruled the fridge out at the very beginning of the investigation. I had not considered taking any sort of macro view in relation to the more minor hypothesis. It wasn't until I had started to consider the seasonal effect of the water table that I stepped back far enough for a wider perspective. Had I considered a wider perspective *in relation to the fridge* then the evaporative action of the drain pan may have come onto my radar much earlier. Frostless fridge-freezers draw out excess condensation and discharges it into a drain pan at the back, keeping your fridge-freezer frost free. The drain pan is designed to be large enough to store excess water until it evaporates. When the device is faulty, the drain pan fills up faster than it is designed for, overflowing. Still, the water will eventually evaporate, then the cycle continues. The speed of the evaporation from the drain pan is subject to change based on the ambient temperature and humidity in the room and behind your fridge. This caused the damp patch to appear and dry cyclically.

The fridge was seven years old and new fridge arrived less than 24 hours later. The carpet hasn't become damp ever since. I sleep soundly in the renewed confidence that my house won't fall into a sink hole. Although, I found plenty of other issues but I remained game to address each myself. For some time, I wondered what the building report on my house would have said because I sure did find a lot that should feature in such a report if I were writing it. I've

Chapter 8: Water

never been more hands on than I have since owning a home, which has highlighted that for all my big problem commercial type thinking, it is not as simple as applying this directly in a residential context (giving credence to RICS proposing in 2024 to create the new chartered title: Chartered Residential Surveyor[10]). I poured some of my first concrete to create a hob wall for a tall fence to be mounted onto (at risk of detailing the entire scope of work, I'll just say the neighbour was uphill from me). My default commercial experience had me overthinking this problem way too much. That said, ODEC can still apply to either. It took an engineer at the office to say it to me straight: "just box and pour it, mate. If you run out of aggregate, just toss in a bunch of rocks or screed from around your yard." It was just a small hob wall after all, and with a render finish, it did what it needed to do and looked the part in the end, perfection is the enemy of done. There's a strange dichotomy that I've often felt looming over me as a building surveyor, a feeling I've discussed and shared with other building surveyors: I was positioned to provide advice on building pathology matters, yet for the longest time I had never so much as laid a brick in my life. There's a lot of value in taking up your own tools every once and a while, especially if you're learning style relies heavily on being practical, testing, and failing. As mentioned previously, YouTube offers unlimited resources such as practical demonstrations and 3D timelapse animations of how everything and anything is built, operates, and repaired.

Much later, the vendor's agent paid us a visit to appraise our home's value. I quizzed him on why the two price drops happened, "the seller had committed to buying another house and needed the cash in a short timeframe." It was about money after all. The biggest purchase you're likely to ever make is buying your home and whilst this topic could fall under a few of the different chapter headings (and constitute books of their own and do), water is probably the most prevailing issue that homes experience. As we've seen, it can come from a variety of sources, and it's path of travel is elusive and concealed. The take away here is this: you should not commit to the purchase of a property without first obtaining a building report from a competent person who has obtained the necessary skills, knowledge and licencing. Buying a property without such a report is a risk that far exceeds the cost to commission the report. It is no different for commercial buyers, be it for the purchase of a small warehouse as part of a retirement investment strategy, or for a multi-million-dollar office tower in the middle of the city as part of a fund manager's portfolio. In a commercial context this report is referred to as a technical due diligence report (TDD). In every case it is money well spent. Even if no significant issues are uncovered the report will provide you with a baseline of the property's condition. Materials deteriorate, warranties expire, and a discerning and diligent owner will plan accordingly. Furthermore, if an issue arises after the fact that should have been identified by the report and was ultimately missed because of incompetence, then the owner has an initial recourse to explore.

What I've just described is broadly applicable throughout the world. It is with regards to standards and licencing requirements where things will begin to differ across territories and jurisdictions. You should have an awareness of the applicable standard or guidance for the report (if there is one), and the qualification or licence requirement for the person undertaking the report. For the purchase of commercial property, it remains relatively straightforward, the industry standard I refer to is applicable globally: The RICS Professional Standard, Technical Due Diligence of Commercial Property 1st Edition, available at rics.org. There is no specific licence requirement to undertake this activity on behalf of commercial clients. Generally speaking, the managers that procure this inspection seek a competent team to undertake it and make their own assessment as to their competence in terms of appropriate qualifications in property, engineering or disciplines related to construction and/or the design of building services. I ask these managers to consider if their consultant is a chartered member of RICS (MRICS or FRICS) who will be across their requirements and bring with them the mark of professionalism.

Chapter 8: Water

For homebuyers commissioning a building report the waters become murky quickly. There are starting points, but receiving one of these reports may raise further questions, since in some cases they are 'say what you see' exercises. They may identify a problem with your speculative purchase, but not how to fix it, or what it might cost. I've provided a table for your reference, which is by no means exhaustive. I've included a sample of territories and jurisdictions. Note, various licencing requirements or a professional qualification may be required by an individual undertaking inspections and reports.

United Kingdom	RICS Home Survey Standard
Australia	Australian Standard 4349.1 Pre-Purchase Residential Inspections inc. Appendix B
United States of America	The American Society of Home Inspectors (ASHI) Standard of Practice and Code of Ethics, and the National Association of Home Inspectors (NAHI) Standards of Practice.
Canada	Canadian Association of Home & Property Inspectors (CAHPI) Standards of Practice
South Africa	South African Home Inspection Training Academy (SAHITA) Standards of Practice.
Hong Kong	No specific standard, however, the Hong Kong Institute of Surveyors (HKIS) provides guidance and standards for building inspections

New Zealand	New Zealand Standard NZS 4306:2005 Residential Property Inspection.
Japan	No specific standard, however, the Japan Association of Home Inspectors (JAHI) provides guidance and standards for home inspections.
Spain	Inspección Técnica de Edificios (ITE), compulsory for buildings over 50 years old.

In any case where you are unsure of requirements, no matter where you are in the world, you can use the 'Find a Surveyor' tool at rics.org to find and contact a Chartered Surveyor close to you. If they aren't able to give you answers I'm certain they'll point you in the right direction. Be water, my friend.

Chapter 9: Deleterious Materials

"Just because something doesn't do what you planned it to do doesn't mean it's useless."

Thomas Edison

Not as commonly used as the word hazardous to describe building materials like asbestos, the word deleterious casts a wider net over materials that deserve equal focus. The dictionary definition of deleterious is: 'causing harm or damage'. In property, a material is considered deleterious when it doesn't perform as expected, is a risk to life, often both.

In Australia, there's confusion between the terms hazardous materials, hazardous substances and dangerous goods; which are sometimes (imprecisely) used interchangeably. 'Hazardous materials' is not well defined, but often relates to materials in buildings or building products.'Hazardous substances' is generally defined in workplace health and safety legislation applicable to each state and territory. Hazardous materials are relatively easy to learn and identify. Where is it, how much of it is there, what is the potential for occupant exposure?

Asbestos may be the most well-known example; a naturally occurring mineral incorporated into materials for not just its high-performing fire-retardant properties but also for its electrical and thermal insulation properties. We incorporated asbestos into anything we could to increase its protection against flame. We mixed it into cement boards. We wove it into sheaths for wiring. We made brake pads for lifts and vehicles out of it. Romans made clothes from it. All the while the natural fibrous composition of asbestos can create microscopic airborne dust that when inhaled can damage your lung tissue. Over time this may cause lung disease, including asbestosis, lung cancer, and mesothelioma. Although asbestos' hazard to health was documented as early as the late 1800s, it took a further 100 years before it was widely regulated. Asbestos Management Plans (AMP) are a typical requirement for buildings and workplaces today. So long as the asbestos that remains in your property is undamaged and undisturbed, there is, generally speaking, a minimal exposure risk. An AMP is designed to monitor this risk by regularly checking the condition of affected elements and implementing appropriate actions. Wearing a mask whilst inspecting any building constructed pre-asbestos bans is a simple and effective inclusion on any risk assessment. The simple act of opening a cupboard or switchboard cabinet can easily reveal the unexpected.

In the United States, efforts to ban the material were frustrated by industry; it was once banned in 1989 and then overturned in 1991. In March 2024, the Biden-Harris Administration finally banned the use of Chrysotile in the United States. This, however, still doesn't change the fate of those that found themselves among clouds of dust in New York City on 9 September 2001. The construction of the ill-fated World Trade Centre was completed in 1971 and asbestos containing materials (ACM) such as cement and textiles were incorporated into both towers. Spray-on asbestos fireproofing material was applied to steel beams along the first 40 floors of the north tower. During its construction, the builder discontinued using asbestos because stricter regulations on the mineral were on the horizon. There were 2,997 fatalities the day the two towers fell but having inhaled various silica dust which undoubtedly included asbestos, people are still dying today as a consequence of the building's collapse. Asbestosis and Mesothelioma symptoms may

Chapter 9: Deleterious Materials

take up to 20 years to develop and are fatal. According to the World Trade Center Health Registry, an estimated 400,000 people were exposed to asbestos on that day.[1]

Importation of asbestos has been banned in Australia since 2004. However, in 2015 an Australian materials company importing their product from China, was discovered by the Australian Border Force to include asbestos. But it was already too late. The material had already made its way throughout the country, affecting up to 70 building sites. It is easy to speculate how, somewhere along a supply chain, the lack of checks and balances may be exploitable by an opportunist that charges a premium for a product and provides something cheaper to pocket the difference. A detective remembers that just because something is declared so, where there is human incentive to get more for less (which there nearly always is), there is always a chance that all is not what it seems.

In the UK, organisations like the British Research Establishment (BRE), and British Board of Agrément (BBA) take responsibility for the testing and certification, respectively, of material performance. BRE's building science research underpins policy decisions and regulation. It became privatised in 1997. They win government contracts for research and arrange different tests for products to say whether they comply or not. BBA gets paid to assess the evidence of tests a product has been through and produces a certificate detailing which standards it met. This includes tests that are conducted over a period of twenty or more years, before obtaining enough comfort that a certain material and its use do not behave in an unexpected way. More than something being simply hazardous to health, deleterious materials remind us that something we thought was a good idea at the time may not stand the test of time (e.g. Lead, mundic, woodwool slabs, polychlorinated biphenyls (PCB) used in fluorescent lighting). Even with research establishments doing the necessary work, sadly, it seems that catastrophe is what it takes to force corporate and government entities to admit inconvenient truths.

The Building Detective

After midnight on Wednesday 14 June 2017, in flat sixteen on the fourth floor of a 24-storey residential tower, an electrical fault in a fridge-freezer began a fire. Behailu Kebede was awakened by an unfamiliar beeping sound that would not stop. He got up to investigate, opening the door to his kitchen to find thick white smoke. He rushed to his living room, grabbed his mobile and at 12:54am called emergency services. By 8:07am the last person was evacuated from the tower. However, not before it was entirely engulfed in flames, killing 72 people, and becoming the worst UK residential fire since World War II.

The fire at Grenfell Tower triggered a public inquiry which commenced May 2018, the purpose of which was to examine the circumstances leading up to and surrounding the fire. The inquiry was divided into phases. Phase 1 established the facts, and phase 2 examined the design, construction and alterations of the tower, it's management, and fire safety. The aim of the inquiry was to identify what needs to be done to prevent a similar disaster from happening again. Importantly, the inquiry was not tasked with identifying if anyone is innocent or guilty, making it separate to a criminal investigation seeking to convict for a range of offences, including corporate manslaughter, fraud, and health and safety offences. Metropolitan Police and Crown Prosecution Service said no charges would be announced until late 2026 at the earliest due to the "complexity" of the inquiry. The inquiry closed after 4 years at the cost of £170 million to the UK taxpayer[2] and published its final report in September 2024, all seven volumes of it. Each volume is in excess of 200 pages.

Chair of the inquiry, Sir Martin Moore-Bick, relied on a team of over forty lawyers to act as his detectives, led by the ferociously inquisitive Richard Millet KC. The cause of the fire is not exactly a mystery, but the specifics which created the circumstances under which it unfolded was unclear. As it normally is with catastrophes there is not a single point of failure; catastrophes are typically caused by multiple points of failure. A series of events coming

Chapter 9: Deleterious Materials

together in such a way that when it strikes it is unstoppable and devastating. Sometimes this is referred to systemic failure, however, that definition refers to multiple failures in a single system whereas various systems, some possibly operating completely independent of one another, possibly with seeds sown as long as fifty years ago, contributed to the Grenfell Tower fire. So many systems and their scale, in fact, was reflected by the inquiry disclosing 320,000 documents and receiving 1,500 witness statements.[3] How did Mr. Millet and his legal team set about identifying each failing for such a catastrophic event? The same way you eat an elephant, one bite at a time.

Behailu Kebede wasn't sure if his kitchen window was open that night, but, like many surviving residents, he stated in is witness statement it was normally kept open all of the time during summer. Whether it was or wasn't, it's clear the fire "jumped" from the kitchen, through an opening, and to the external cladding of the tower. Less than a year before the fire, the tower was refurbished. This included the installation of an external building envelope made from aluminium sandwich panels; two aluminium sheets, with a polyethylene core. Polyethylene is the polymer holding the two aluminium sheets together. It so happens that polyethylene is as flammable as petrol. When the fire jumped out of Behailu's flat window, it really didn't take much to set the entire building on fire, overwhelming its occupants, and outpacing the London Fire Brigade (LFB). There are a great number of systems, steps, initiatives, protocols, regulations, management practices, and statutory requirements that exist to prevent a fire like this from ever being allowed to occur. Then why was it that it did occur, even after two London fires, one Melbourne fire and one Dubai fire, with similar hallmarks, occurring in the decade leading up to Grenfell? Lakanal House in 2009, where a faulty TV caused a fire in a 12-storey residential building, which was allowed to spread because of unsafe refurbishment works; Shepherd's Court in 2016 where a faulty tumble drier caused a fire in a 20-storey residential building, which cladding contributed to the vertical spread of the fire, affecting several floors above; Lacrosse Apartments in 2014, a 23-storey residential building in Melbourne in which cladding contributed to the vertical spread of fire; and Address Downtown, Dubai, in 2015 an electrical short circuit caused a fire which spread vertically across it's cladding (even though it was 2013 when the UAE revised its building safety code to require that cladding on all new buildings over 15 metres tall be fire-resistant). There were other fires, of course, however, these in particular were high profile, included media coverage and subsequently were difficult to ignore.

As the inquiry progressed, one by one, each point of failure at Grenfell Tower revealed themselves. Whilst the aluminium composite panels (ACP[†]) or affected cladding may receive a lot of focus due to its dramatic infamy of being highly combustible, it would be careless to consider it the primary and sole cause of what happened. Here's just a sample of the observations and deductions:

- There was national guidance that determined the building's evacuation procedure which in this case was to "stay put". Typically, buildings are designed to be compartmentalised against the spread of fire, and for a tall residential tower the default safety protocol is to remain in your dwelling since any outbreak is expected to be limited to one compartment for it to be extinguished by the attending firefighters. This being the status quo for protection against fire, firefighters are not even trained in the partial or full evacuation of a high-rise residential building. Ultimately existing procedures inhibited a decision to fully evacuate, costing lives. The stay put policy is predicated on the assumption that occupants can stay safe in their apartment from a fire contained within a single compartment somewhere else in the building without being affected by flames, heat or smoke.

[†] referred to throughout the inquiry as ACM: aluminium composite material. However, the acronym ACM has long been used to mean asbestos containing materials, so we'll refer to the cladding as ACP here.

Chapter 9: Deleterious Materials

- Compartmentation failed. It's an important layer of protection gives robustness to the stay put policy, that no other layer of protection can provide. Any breach of the compartmentation makes evacuation the preferred option. Not only did the fire "jump" out of a window, find fuel to escape compartmentation and continue its path of travel, it was also revealed that many of the doors replaced during the refurbishment did not meet fire safety standards. An adequately performing fire door is designed to resist a fire and stop its spread for at least 30 minutes. These doors are referred to as FR30 or FR60, as in, a door having a fire rating of 30 or 60 minutes. Furthermore, compartmentalisation relies on penetrations being 'fire stopped'. Penetrations are holes made in walls, ceilings and floors to reticulate services like electricity cabling, plumbing and gas lines. Fire stopping is the method of closing any holes and gaps with a suitable fire-retardant material, like expanding flame retardant foam or fire pillows. The inquiry found the building had inadequate fire stopping throughout.

- uPVC window frames, a robust material that's difficult to burn, loses its mechanical strength at low temperatures, melting between 75 and 105 degrees and behaving like gum, which is expected to have happened between 5 and 11 minutes after the fire started. Windows failed exposing combustible materials beneath it. Expert witness Professor José Torero did not think the detail of which material ignited first is important, but rather the principle that a small fire would have been able to ignite any of these materials, putting into motion the events of the night.[4]

- There was an issue with the building's smoke ventilation system, which is supposed to ventilate smoke in the event of a fire, especially away from the fire escape stairwell. Inhaling smoke is the primary cause of death during a fire, and the cause for the majority of resident's deaths at Grenfell, be it because they attempted to escape through toxic smoke, or that they followed the 'stay put' advice and the smoke had reached them before the late order to evacuate was made (or that the order to get out was not received at all as there was no communication system to rely information to residents).

- The width of the only fire escape stairwell was narrow, as testified by firefighters wearing breathing apparatus (BA) kit, which includes a tank worn on their back. The stairwell was so tight that it did not allow two firefighters wearing BA kit to quickly pass each other, relying on backing themselves into a corner to let another pass. Nor did the stairwell width help firefighters carry casualties down stairs, whose feet and legs kept getting stuck in the stair railing. One testimony described how a casualty lying lifeless on the stairs created a trip hazard, worsened by the stairs being filled with thick toxic smoke reducing all visibility. The firefighter attempted to move her for the safety of everyone else but couldn't as they found her leg to be caught and twisted in the rail.[5]

- The cladding had already accelerated the fire spread, but to add to firefighters woes, blue fire was observed to areas on the tower, indicating that gas lines had been compromised, now contributing to the fire. The local gas authority had already been contacted to cut the main gas line to the building, but all too late.

- Building plans weren't made available, there was no "premises information box", and plans couldn't be obtained from the local authority. Floor numbers were not indicated at all within stairwells, in some limited cases they had been drawn on by hand. Making it overall difficult to navigate the building.

- The dry riser outlet, an empty water pipe which runs up the inside of the building, was located at the furthest point away from the ground floor lobby door. That meant that any lift lobby that was compromised by fire, firefighters couldn't connect their hose to the dry riser unless that fire was put out, which would be time consuming. If crews connect hose to too many floors, the water pressure drops making it unusable.

Chapter 9: Deleterious Materials

They tried to remedy this situation by running additional hoses up the only staircase, from a fire engine parked outside. Crews were getting soaked with water as they travelled up the stairs, then entering a fire compartment and getting "boiled". At one stage falling debris cut the hose supply outside.

- Emergency lighting failed, or rather, where there was lighting, the thickness and colour of the smoke rendered them useless, forcing firefighters and casualties to "feel" their way to escape.

- The firefighters radios failed once they had ascended the building, losing contact with coordination crews on the ground (this is also something that occurred to firefighters entering the World Trade Centre in 2001, with American fire and building codes developed by 2009 requiring coverages to be supported by installing radio repeater technology.[6]) Amid the rapidly changing, unprecedented situation, firefighters resorted to passing handwritten notes to each other regarding intel received from fire survival guidance calls (or FSGs; the calls received by 999, the UK's emergency services phone number, from residents trapped by fire, heat or smoke).

- There was a lack of sprinklers in the tower, which up to that point were not a requirement in UK residential tower buildings.

- In the sum experience of firefighters, some with twenty-plus years tenure, individuals had experienced receiving up to just two FSGs for a single incident. The 999 operations centres were overwhelmed with multiple calls, under resourced to efficiently filter FSGs to the fireground. Calls began to be diverted to operation centres in Manchester and Kent, as many as thirty at once. Most operators had perhaps experienced a single FSG call in their career. The night of the fire produced a total 176 FSG calls. Information was not able to be relayed effectively to the fireground, which missed rescue opportunities. The enquiry was able to demonstrate how this specific issue resulted in the loss of a family of five people in one flat.

- During the design of the refurbishment, a value engineering exercise, an exercise in identifying opportunities to save money through substituting materials or making minor amendments to the design, saw the replacement of the cladding with the combustible material that was eventually installed. Expert witness Professor Luke Bisby said the cladding failed to meet building regulation requirements, which states that external walls to buildings should adequately resist the spread of fire.[7]

- Materials manufacturer, Celotex, over engineered a full-scale fire test in a deliberate attempt to create a misleading test report. A shortened version of the report was used when customers pressed, which omitted details of the use of magnesium oxide. The misleading test report showed a rebranded product marketed as being suitable for use on buildings over 18 metres. It also copied the sales literature of their commercial rival, Kingspan. Kingspan also engaged in misleading marketing and looked for ways around the testing to help their product become widely adopted throughout the UK. When counsel put to Kingspan "you're trying to push the BBA as far as possible that are going to maximise the sales of K15, even if they're not true. That's right, isn't it?" Kingspan's representative replied, "That's right, yes."

- BRE's impartiality was brought into question. BRE admitted on relying on the honesty of the client when then was no security in the burn hall, allowing clients to sneak materials onto their rigs to help them pass.

- The inquiry even went so far as to question how, if at all, institutional, unconscious or subconscious racism played its part in contributing to the conditions that led to the disaster.

The highest-ranking officer in attendance that night, LFB Commissioner, Dany Cotton, had previously been the Director of

Chapter 9: Deleterious Materials

Safety and Assurance at the LFB.[8] Such a role demands an expertise in assessing risk. Part of undertaking a risk assessment is essentially dreaming up likely and unlikely hazardous occurrences, then documenting and putting in place plans to downgrade or completely eliminate those risks. On Grenfell she said, "The whole of the system of that night, of what happened to that building would have been deemed to have been a completely unrealistic scenario that would never happen." This was the basis of her argument that firefighters would never have received training on how to deal with something like Grenfell, dismissing it as unrealistic, "we wouldn't develop training for something that simply shouldn't happen."[9]

But it did happen. I make this point, not to examine whether LFB missed the signs that should have signalled to them to consider training for some kind of unrealistic, worst-case scenario (the inquiry found plenty of signs) but to serve as a stark reminder to everyone. No matter how many deductions or scenarios you've dreamed of, however unlikely they may be, you must remain open to the possibility that you have not thought of everything and devise backstops. Known unknowns refer to "risks you are aware of, such as cancelled flights,"[10] whereas unknown unknowns are risks that come from situations that are so unexpected that they would not be considered. Chris Voss says in *Never Split the Difference*, "To uncover these unknowns, we must interrogate our world, must put out a call, and intensely listen to the response. Ask lots of questions."

Information heard by the inquiry, certainly to the ears of the bereaved and survivors, was technical and complicated, but necessary. They are the building blocks that help everyone understand what came next but to the bereaved and survivors it is not surprising that the level of detail would have felt overwhelming at times. Ultimately, they want to know why their loved ones died. The enquiry uncovered so many reasons. Of course, one of those reasons is something caused a fire to start in the first place. For something that starts so small and becomes destructive beyond all recognition, a forensic level of problem solving is required. ODEC is applied in layers and layers within the Grenfell Inquiry, but most of all we can see how carefully it is applied to confirm Behailu's Kebede's declaration that it was indeed a faulty fridge-freezer that started the fire. Expert witness Duncan Glover, a specialist in investigating electrical fires, delivered his findings to the enquiry.[11]

Observations

- Behailu saw light coloured smoke coming from the general area of the fridge-freezer next to the kitchen window, rising up from the floor coming towards him.
- Photographs and video of the fire that Behailu had taken, and photos taken by investigators afterwards, show burn patterns which could be interpreted by experts.
- The only place firefighters found evidence of burning was in Behailu's kitchen.
- Following the fire, on inspection of the consumer unit in Behailu's flat, it was evident that two circuits had turned off automatically ("tripped") and would have had to do so before Behailu switched off the power as he left.
- The circuit breaker is designed to detect a short circuit.
- A bread maker used in traditional Ethiopian cooking was discovered in the flat.
- Short circuits with enough current can cause arcing, where electricity travels through air.
- 27 days after the fire, a piece of wire with 24 strands exhibiting arc damage, was found in one of the bedrooms.
- There is a history of two previous fires where the same model of fridge-freezer was linked.

Chapter 9: Deleterious Materials

Deductions

- The refurbishment was a continued source of contention between residents and the tenant management organisation (TMO). There is a need to rule out that fire was started deliberately.
- Behailu may have been cooking using the cooker, starting the fire from non-electrical means using cooking oil.
- If combustible material is in close proximity to where ever there is arcing, it's possible this can occur before the circuit detects the issue and automatically switches off.
- Photographs and video showing the pattern of damage usually leads back to the area of worst damage. As a general rule, the fire started where there is an area of most damage, ruling out the majority and focusing on a small area. The imagery showed this small area to be the fridge, deducing the fridge caused the fire.
- In fighting the fire, the flats were inundated with water. It's possible that the arc damaged wire found in the bedroom floated there and belongs to the faulty appliance which started the fire, therefore identifying and confirming the cause of the start of the fire.
- The manufacturer of the fridge-freezer proposed that a lit cigarette was thrown through the window of the fourth floor flat (noting the enquiry points out that this theory is not based on any observations or evidence provided to the enquiry).

Elimination

- Sniffer dogs trained to detect petrol augmented the senses of investigators. They did not discover anything to indicate the fire was started deliberately.

- The fluorescent ceiling light in the kitchen and it's wiring did not exhibit any arc damage, or "evidence of abnormal electrical activity."
- The switches for the 4 cooker hobs were all found in the off position, giving enough confidence that the cooker was not in use at the time the fire started. The cooker, which only exhibited superficial damage, was connected to a different circuit to the one which tripped, eliminating the cooker as the cause.
- The bread maker's power supply cord was found to be intact, including the plug and fuse, concluding with enough confidence that it was not connected at the time the fire started.
- All appliances in the kitchen connected to circuit 7 were examined to identify which the arc damaged wire might come from. The extractor fan was on circuit 7. On inspection the fuse for the fan had not blown. In his position as expert witness, Mr. Glover confirmed a 3amp fuse will always blow more quickly than a 32amp fuse, therefore eliminating the extractor fan as the cause.
- An arc damaged wire was found inside the freezer. In Behailu's witness statement, he notes that it stopped working nine years ago and that a fridge technician confirmed it's fuse had blown. For this reason, it had remained unplugged since then, therefor concluding the damage to this freezer occurred well before the night of the fire.
- The large fridge-freezer was connected to circuit 7, and its wiring within the appliance's relay compartment matched that of the arc-damaged wire found in the bedroom. A CT scan found inadequate crimping of these wires. Evidence provided by a further expert witness, Professor Naimh Nic Dade, spoke to burn patterns observed to the fridge-freezer, showing how the whole appliance caught fire on the night.

Chapter 9: Deleterious Materials

Conclusion

We've seen time and time again that it is in fact difficult to reach a nice, neat, wrapped-up conclusion. For this reason, it is important to be clear. Mr. Glover makes this caveat at the enquiry, "nothing is 100% certain. Based on all my training, experience investigating electrical fires, my conclusions are to a reasonable degree of engineering certainty. Most probable." Professor Nic Dade also noted that, whilst she concluded the cause of the fire was electrical in origin, which components remained, in her view, undetermined.[12]

Having considered all the possibilities, investigating each through a process of closer examination, going so far as augmenting smell using dogs and augmenting sight using medical scanning technology, it was with a high degree of probability that Mr. Glover spoke his conclusion into the enquiry's evidence: Poorly crimped wires within the fridge-freezer are likely to have caused overheating, getting worse over time of being unaddressed, igniting the wire's PVC sheaths (which ignites at around 90 degrees), starting a small fire inside the fridge-freezer's relay compartment. Unsheathed wires which should not have touched came into contact with each other creating a short circuit, tripping circuit breaker 7. Noting, however the breaker tripping was too late. The fire had already started.

Let's not forget, expert witness Professor José Torero noting the principle that any small fire near a window at Grenfell Tower would have put into motion the events of the night. For anyone who loses a loved one, we naturally want to know how they died. We know that inhaling asphyxiating smoke caused most people to die at Grenfell. Obviously, this is not a good answer as it is not the whole story. A deleterious material like ACP allowing rapid fire to spread, is how they died. The fridge that started the fire is how they died. Every decision that led to the woeful refurbishment of the tower is how they died. What if the field of observational view was expanded even further? In *Show Me the Bodies* Peter Apps goes as far to suggest that government policy in the 1960s, is how they died. He argues that policy decisions first evidenced by the 1968 collapse of an east London tower block, Ronan Point, contain the seeds of attitudes and behaviours that continue to fester up to present day.[13] Finally, in February 2025, the UK government concluded Grenfell Tower will be "sensitively deconstructed" following the eighth anniversary of the fire.

For the uninitiated curious about the machinations of the construction industry, one could do worse than listening to the Grenfell Inquiry Podcast offered by BBC. I heavily relied upon it to write this case study. The podcast covered the inquiry for every day it sat, clearly breaking down and communicating technical language and concepts. This is not casual listening, however. At times it's heartbreaking. That said, I can't understate enough that I believe every industry professional should get to know the detail of this particular inquiry, for it revealed apparently unchecked, insidious and plainly ignorant behaviour at nearly every conceivable layer. It must have repercussions on how we operate. We are likely to have witnessed or experienced some of this behaviour first hand at some point in our careers. The inquiry's cast of characters, especially those introduced in Phase 2, which included the materials suppliers and various consultants, painted a bleak picture of ethical and moral failings; an unwillingness to take responsibility. Many actions were driven by commercial gain and a complete disregard for safety. Mr. Millet requested that witnesses abstain from "a merry go round of buck passing," and sadly, that is exactly what followed. Every "I do not recall," "in hindsight" and "on reflection I perhaps shouldn't have," is likely to have reinforced the public's view that property and construction industry is driven by unethical behaviour, where no one is willing to take responsibility for their actions. In my view this is more a reflection of sales culture, and not the culture of property professionals, but the two are unavoidably linked. Professionalism relies heavily on ethics. The inquiry revealed an underbelly of self-preservation, not self-sacrifice to preserve others. Accepting risk contractually is not good enough. Owning responsibility, acting morally and ethically against commercial interest, in the interest of the safety of others is what we aspire to.

RAAC

Whilst in practice there is an expectation that a certain thing is not the domain of a certain party to consider, e.g., the architect should be aware of the properties of ACP. The Grenfell Inquiry showed us how an architect might wash their hands of any duty of care. After all, contractually the risk lies with the design and build contractor. The inquiry exposed this lack of ethics and even narrow mindedness. This is not unique to the Grenfell case. Take the case of RAAC, or reinforced, aerated autoclave concrete.

In 1924, architect and inventor Dr. Johan Axel Eriksson working with Professor Henrik Kreüger at the Royal Institute of Technology, Sweden, patented RAAC: reinforced aerated autoclave concrete. Their organisation, Yxhults Ånghärdade Gasbetong became the first registered building materials brand in the world. Later, cellular concrete brand, Hebel, opened its first plant in Germany in 1943. Today Hebel continues to manufacture and sell RAAC, their website claiming to be Australia's leading manufacturer of autoclaved aerated concrete. Hebel describes their RAAC products as "a strong yet lightweight building product that is available in panels or blocks. It is kind to the environment, quick to build with and better to live in."[14]

Almost 100 years after RAAC was patented, UK kids rejoiced as the government announced to extend their long summer holiday. Of course that's not how they worded it. At the start of September 2023, the UK government announced around 100 schools wouldn't be able to reopen following the long summer holiday until safety measures had been implemented to address the risks of building collapse. RAAC was used in their construction. The hysteria quickly spread beyond the UK. Governments sought status updates from relevant departments responsible for portfolios of public sector properties. Do we have this? Are we at risk? How quickly do we need to act?

Older RAAC is mainly found in roofs, occasionally in floors and walls, in public sector buildings like schools, hospitals, airports, housing blocks, theatres and other public buildings constructed between the 1940s and 1980s. If you ever needed any insight into why our industry uses so many acronyms, here it is: RAAC.

- Reinforced: it contains steel reinforcement bars to provide strength against tension.
- Autoclaved: It's made in an autoclave, a machine used to carry out industrial and scientific processes requiring elevated temperature and pressure.
- Aerated: Instead of relying on heavy coarse aggregate (the bigger stones that fill out concrete), it contains a high volume of air. Small air bubbles make up the body of the concrete, a cellular structure offering strength whilst remaining lightweight.
- Concrete: a building material made from cement mix and water.

RAAC has some really great performance characteristics. It is really great at resisting fire and mould. It offers good thermal and acoustic insulation. It doesn't spall or delaminate. Hand tools could be used to manually drive mechanical fixings into it. Eventually RAAC fell out of favour in the 1980s and it was soon identified as deleterious by the BRE. We have long been aware of this material, its properties, and how to manage it in situ when it is undamaged, undisturbed, and considered low risk in its overall context.

In 1994 the UK Department of Education asked BRE to inspect two flat roofs of schools in Essex reported to exhibit ponding water and excessive cracking to their undersides or soffits. Their inspections found excessive deflections which caused water to pond. BRE published research papers in December 1996 which described

Chapter 9: Deleterious Materials

excessive deflections and cracking had been identified in a number of RAAC roof planks and highlighted "excessive" issues in a significant number of older buildings using the material. The useful life of RAAC was considered to be 30 years, so this was consistent in especially older constructions, at the height of RAAC's popularity between 1940s and 1960s.

Just like today's modern concrete, the steel reinforcement bar in RAAC becomes vulnerable to corrosion. However, due to its lightweight form, the expansion of the corroding steel is enough to suddenly compromise it without any warning; collapsing under a load it can no longer carry. RAAC remained out the public eye until 2018:

- 2018: The roof of Singlewell Primary School in Gravesend, Kent UK, collapsed over a weekend because of RAAC failing.
- 2021: A ceiling collapsed at Rosemead Preparatory School in Dulwich, South East London – a teacher and fifteen pupils were injured.
- June 2023: The UK National Audit Office (NAO) published the Condition of school buildings report which identified 572 schools might have RAAC present.
- July 2023: Another collapse in a school building – previously not thought to have been at risk – is reported.
- September 2023: The government announced 100 schools will be contacted before the new school term began.

So even though this isn't a new issue, following a long period of apparent inaction and a fear that nothing was being done, it received a flurry of media attention, creating a sense of urgency. A sudden influx of public pressure from school groups, activists, lobbyists, caused politicians to react.

The status quo around this material hasn't changed. We know it exists, we know how to identify it, assess it, and what recommendations to make, just as we do for all other deleterious materials. Context is important. The Hebel I mentioned before continues to manufacture and sell RAAC today. Their website shows how one of their products is appropriate for corridor walls. We must consider the manufacturer's intent and appropriateness for the use of their product and if that reflects how it is actually being used. More likely than not, it is being used responsibly and as intended. We follow the same process we've always followed: when a risk is identified, we run it to ground and we can use ODEC for a comprehensive analysis.

BRE Information Paper 10/96 contains helpful detail for building surveyors on how to identify RAAC together with suggested maintenance measures. This was updated in 2002 to Information Paper 7/2002. Other historic resources include the European Standard EN 12602:2008 which was withdrawn in 2013.

3D Printed Buildings

3D printing technology in construction purports to significantly reduce costs and construction time, enhance efficiency, and reduce waste. Building-scale printers work the same way as regular ones. They deposit thin layers of material over previous layers, until the form is finished. 3D printing has been around since the 1980s but in today's construction industry it is known as *additive manufacturing*. It has proven to be an effective, efficient way to make complex parts and shapes. Such as formwork for non-standard concrete shapes, and mechanical parts for wind turbines, which previously had to be manufactured offsite and awkwardly transported to their new home.

When it comes to squeezing cement mix out from an industrial piping bag, there are still important variables to consider. Inconsistent quality of printing can lead to structural weaknesses. Structures may suffer from weak points, especially at the layer interfaces, so by the time it's all layered together like an unappetising grey spekkoek it's difficult to ensure uniform strength and stability is consistent throughout the entire structure.

Chapter 9: Deleterious Materials

Concrete is well known for its fire-resistant properties, again as a result of decades of thorough testing and certification. A project located in California used a special concrete mix together with additive manufacturing to construct an accessory dwelling unit (ADU). A habitable structure located on the same property as the primary residence. The aim of the ADU is to withstand Californian wildfires. It features concrete walls and a steel roof and avoided combustible materials like timber and mechanical fixings to reduce the risk of fire penetration.[15] The assertion that concrete is fire-resistant in this case might arise from a case of conventional wisdom. However, consider for a moment that the way the cement is piped in layers may affect how the layers bind. Cracks and failure characteristics under these conditions are not well documented. In 2016, Dubai claimed to print 25% of its buildings by 2023.[16] A fairly lofty goal, since revised to 2030. Determined to be the 3D printing leader of the construction world however, in February 2024 Dubai issued their first licence for construction using 3D printing technology for buildings.[17] In this case it was for a private villa.

The long-term performance of these structures remains speculative. While 3D printing/additive manufacturing offers promising advantages, the durability and safety of the materials under real-world conditions need further exploration. The future of 3D printed buildings hinges on balancing innovation with safety, ensuring that advancements do not come at the cost of life safety.

Aircrete

My wife showed me a short news report by Channel 7 about a couple located on the Sunshine Coast QLD building their dream home out of a material called aircrete. The reporter doted, "curves are in all the right places to make sure it lasts," with reference to the structure's hobbit-esque dome appearance. The owner-builder couple apparently having obtained council approval, claimed that the material they exclusively used to build their home was termite proof, cyclone proof, and fire resistant. All from using a mixture of general-purpose cement and …washing up liquid. My wife examined me for a reaction. Being a creative person, she was coming from a place that agreed "isn't this clever?" Cheekily though she was baiting me to shoot it down. I had to tread carefully.

Each time you read about an innovative new construction material or approach, you also have to consider the potential for it to be a future deleterious material. Of course we need to explore better ways to do things, but it must not be at the expense of compromising life safety in the future. The development of new materials and practices requires the patience needed to examine performance over at least a 20-year period, ideally more. In a world experiencing a fourth industrial revolution and one that demands a sink or swim attitude, the conditions under which we can practice this patience are wearing thin. Construction sciences have amassed enough examples of deleterious materials for us to readily refer to, to know that going all in on something like aircrete is a risk. I'm not a gambling man, but if building your forever home primarily out of a material you can't demonstrate will withstand twenty cycles of four changing seasons isn't going all in, then I'm not sure what is.

Improvement still relies on innovation, experimentation, and even happy accidents. The kind where no one gets hurt and something positive emerges. Cement wasn't originally meant to revolutionise construction. In 1824, Joseph Aspdin created it to mimic the high-quality stone quarried on the Isle of Portland, England.

Façade Glazing Inclusions

The site of what was once Brisbane's original port dating back to 1879 is occupied by One Eagle, Brisbane (formally Waterfront Place); a concrete framed, fully glazed, 40-storey commercial office tower constructed in 1989. It was the location of my first project after I moved to Brisbane in 2013; the refurbishment of Hon. Bill Hayden AC's office, the 21st governor-general of Australia. In June 2015, the building was bought by Dexus Property Group for $635 million AUD.[18] When Dexus purchased it, they didn't have to rely

Chapter 9: Deleterious Materials

on the technical due diligence report to unearth the issue with it's glazing. News outlets had well documented the glazed panels which had been exploding off the side of the building since 1990.

A nickel sulphide inclusion is one of over fifty types of glass inclusion, naturally formed impurities created from the glass making process. This type of inclusion is a problem in fully tempered glass which is designed to break into hundreds of small cubes. Through glass fractography, the study of broken glass to understand failures, analysts found at the vocal point of the break created by a nickel sulphide inclusion, there's a different pattern: a pair of multi-sided figures next to each other that look like a butterfly. Between the border of these two polygons is a tiny dot. Barely visible to the human eye, that little dot is responsible for spontaneously exploding the entire sheet of glass in an instant. This shattering symphony takes place at over 4,800km/h or 3,000mph, all coming from one small inclusion that can be between 0.0762 millimetres and 0.381 millimetres wide. Temperature causes the inclusion to grow in size, eventually breaking the glass. They are too small to be detected in the manufacturing process. There is currently no technology that eliminates the possible formation of nickel sulphide stones in glass. There are, however, controls that glass manufacturers implement to greatly reduce the likelihood of inclusions, like avoiding the use of nickel in any primary batch formations, banning nickel baring metals from all operations, and by using special plant and equipment such as magnetic separators.

Whilst it's not possible to identify on a building inspection using the naked eye, where there are concerns which indicate a possible risk, possible inclusions can be identified using polarised light, or a photographic method which can be used to help identify possible inclusions. By using an appropriate macro lens at a resolution that will allow significant magnification. Being able to adequately collect and examine these images enters the realm of a construction science specialist. Glass manufacturers maintain that the risk of nickel sulphide inclusions forming is very small, estimating that incidents are 1 in 13,000kg of glass. One Eagle drew the short straw.

Between 1990 and 1997, One Eagle documented around 140 spontaneous failures, and on 68 of those occasions the nickel sulphide inclusion located at the initiation point was able to be recovered, analysed, and measured. The tower contains around 9,500 individual panes of glass, 4,194 of which were subject to a photographic investigation process which identified 53,594 inclusions, 291 of which were identified as nickel sulphide within 281 windows.[19] Around 120 higher risk panes were replaced as part of a $1.6 million project.[20] Re-cladding the entire building was not financially or operationally feasible. Instead, as well as maintaining discreet exclusion zones at the base of the property, large canopies and shade sails were installed around the base of the building. To look at the port cochere and surrounding shading, one would think these are architecturally interesting and practical features sheltering visitors and vehicles from the hot Queensland sun and monsoon like rains. Whilst this is true, they have a far more important job: to protect those below by catching falling glass whenever a panel unexpectedly explodes.

The precinct, named Waterfront Brisbane, is set to continue to transform the city with the approval of a $2.5 billion AUD development which includes two new office towers, a riverfront retail precinct and expanded public space, including the widening of the riverwalk and a new destination dining experience. The development's scheduled completion is 2028. Progress marches on.

PART III: Continual Professional Development

The final part of this book explores additional knowledge areas for today's building consultant, including focusing on a selection of modern challenges that lie before the profession. If Part II is grounded in timeless skills of critical thinking and problem solving, the heart of Part III is about having an awareness of the challenges of the present and future.

Chapter 10: Building Services, Code Compliance & Contaminated Land

You can't handle the truth!

Colonel Nathan R. Jessup, *A Few Good Men*

For a building consultant to hand over as complete a picture as possible of a property, they must work together with a group of multidisciplinary specialists. Together, the team can piece together the puzzle as far as reasonably possible to determine the sum total of the *physical* risks that may exist when buying land and property. I say physical to make the distinction between this and financial, accounting, legal and operational risks that surface during due diligence, and fall into the domains of accountants, lawyers, and other analysts.

Each specialist in the property consultancy team benefits from a solid understanding of their colleague's specialisms. This way they are able to work cohesively and recognise when to defer to each other's expertise. It is also critical to understand what lies outside your area of competency. That's what this chapter is about, technical due diligence in the context of buying and selling property of a commercial scale. This includes, but is not limited to, office towers, warehousing, retail, manufacturing and high-density residential. Further to the involvement of a building consultant, there can also be a façade abseiler, site boundary surveyor and town planner. Depending on what your needs are, you may not need any of these at all. Let's examine three key areas that must not be overlooked.

Building Services

A building without services is little more than a static shell. A hut or treehouse by another name. In terms of its performance characteristics, without building services a building is limited to aspiring to be water and wind tight and remain standing for at least fifty years. And that's about it! It's the building services that bring the empty husk to life.

Hark back to Chapter 7 when I said buildings move, even breathe. Let's go a step further. Imagine a building as a living, breathing organism. The mechanical services act as the building's lungs; with room sized boxes called air handling units, and a system of mechanically moving parts, like, fans, actuators and motors, providing fresh air through ventilation ducts and air conditioning systems. Car-sized cylinders called chillers function like sweat glands, working to dissipate heat and keep the building's temperature regulated. Hydraulic or plumbing services represent the building's circulatory system, with plumbing and water management systems delivering water for drinking and sanitation, while efficiently removing waste. Pressure systems release excess pressure ...preventing any unexpected "explosions." Prescribed fire safety systems represent the building's immune system, with detection, alarms, sprinklers, and fire extinguishers in place to combat any threats. Central to everything is the Building Management System (BMS), a computer which functions as the brain. Attached to this computer is a vast network of ethernet cables connecting sensors like nerves, all together acting as the central nervous system. Monitoring and even autonomously controlling the performance of

Chapter 10: Building Services, Code Compliance & Contaminated Land

plant and equipment, reporting it all back to the brain. Finally, it is the people inside that are the lifeblood of the building, moving around and making it truly alive. Its beating heart.

People inside the building need to be in control of their environment to remain happy and comfortable. They can control the temperature no matter the time of year or in which climate they live. They can illuminate the inside when it is dark outside. They can bring hot and cold water inside and send all wastewater outside without carrying it or opening any doors. It can transport its occupants from one part of the building to another. Not only can the building protect itself from fire, but it can also protect itself from physical and digital intruders. It's fair to say that far more can go wrong with a building's services than its structure. And depending on the activities taking place inside that building, the risks can escalate very quickly:

- During Hurricane Sandy in 2012, backup generators failed at major New York hospitals due to flooding, causing a critical loss of power.[1] This failure revealed vulnerabilities in the placement and protection of essential systems against natural disasters.

- Most data centres have backup power to protect IT equipment in the event of a power outage. Typically, it involves the use of uninterruptible power supplies (UPSs) to sustain operations until generators kick in. That's all well and good, but if the data centre's cooling system is not similarly accounted for, the IT equipment may suffer outages anyway as you're going to have one hot data centre. If a data centre experienced a power outage that knocked the chiller plant offline, it would result in a rapid temperature rise within the facility. The lack of backup power for the cooling system would cause numerous servers to overheat and shut down, leading to substantial financial losses and service disruptions.

- University buildings often represent aged building stock and as such, an elevated risk brought forth from aged building services. A room-sized boiler may supply hot water to multiple campus buildings, including residences. Failures are often traced back to poor maintenance and delayed replacement of aging equipment. In this scenario, facilities managers would likely have to implement temporary heating solutions and expedite the installation of new boilers to restore normal operations, all at what would otherwise be an avoidable cost if planned for in advance.

The financial risk associated with simply having to buy replacement equipment should come across as fairly obvious to most, things like chillers and lifts are very big-ticket items indeed. However, the overall risks expand far beyond replacement cost alone. Consider the replacement themselves are likely to represent complex projects that must be delivered by competent professionals. Considerations include: the time required to plan, procure and contract these projects; the operational impact to all tenant-customers; the likelihood of a rent relief clause in their leases for any disruptions; the lead times and costs to apply for road closures; successfully obtaining an airspace licence from your neighbours so that you have adequate oversailing rights for your crane to swing over them. The list goes on. For a property fund that is supposed to return reliable dividends, or a business making money for its investors and owners, this is all a bit of a nightmare.

A professional that finds themselves working broadly across all of these services likely didn't start out that way. There is no qualification for "all building services" consultant (though there's some great and very technical textbooks which cover this broad area). Generally, a person may have started their career in one area, as a plumber, an electrician, or a mechanical engineer. Next thing they know, one of these roles leads to an opportunity to manage a building. Often, showing competence and experience in a core area, and a willingness to learn, can be entry into a profession as a facility manager. It's similar for those building services professionals who find themselves providing technical due diligence services as a consultant. If they didn't come from a background of managing buildings, then it's likely they came in as a specialist in one area, then learned the ropes in all the others with support from specialist colleagues in the wider team. When I worked for a property company, my manager had spent part of his career as a mechanical engineer in the merchant navy before becoming chief engineer of a hotel building. He would say "why not? Hotels are like big ships that don't move around. They've got all the same stuff in 'em."

Building Code Compliance

Professionals in this field typically assume one of two roles: someone who checks building work at various points during construction work in order to provide a certificate to allow occupation; or someone who inspects existing buildings to primarily provide advisory and consultancy services. We'll focus on the latter.

When buying a building many of the potential code compliance risks include inadequate travel distance to fire escapes, hand rail heights, lack of tactile ground surface indicators, to name just a few. Concerns examine the full gambit of the building code. The challenge that many end up having however, is that a building, while more than likely to have complied at the time of construction, is unlikely to comply with *current* building standards. However, the existing building does not necessarily have to be brought up to code. Not unless it is compelled to do so. Under some circumstances, if an older building is subject to a major refurbishment and it's determined that it represents changing more than 50% of the building, then it may trigger a requirement to pay for the entire building to be upgraded to meet present day code. Depending on what a purchaser's plans are for a building, this is a delicate risk to balance. In Australia there is not a strict trigger percentage, and many factors are considered by multiple parties. The decision to bring certain elements up to code may be a commercial one, purely to downgrade a liability risk, like the risk of someone being injured and making a claim against the owner. Though again, it's not a mandatory requirement.

The consultant will also identify what performance solutions there are and ensure they haven't been compromised. A performance solution is something that is engineered as an alternative to being able to meet the code, and formally certified. Following the Grenfell disaster many parts of the world finally started waking up to the risk presented by combustible materials on the sides of buildings. Queensland was the only state or territory in Australia to legislate by amending the Building Regulation 2006 (now superseded by the Building Regulation 2021). New laws which commenced in 2018 required building owners meeting specific conditions to register with the Government and participate in a three-stage *Safer Buildings* process. Owners were given deadlines to complete each stage, with the third and final stage completed by 2021. The whole process was closed by 2023. What did owners have to do, exactly?

Suddenly there were thousands of privately owned buildings that potentially did not meet the code, *and* they were now required by legislation to assess their building to declare to the government whether or not they were affected. The owner was then placed in the position of deciding what to do to comply going forward. Display an "affected private building notice" next to their public entrance for all to see for a period of seven years, *or* remove and replace all the non-compliant materials, *or* implement a performance solution (an engineered alternative to compliance). And yes, the owner had to pay for whatever choice they made.

Performance solutions aren't unusual things, but they aren't trivial either. In QLD, often Queensland Fire Department are involved as well as the certifier, since they are the ones that have to run into the burning building after all. Obtaining a performance solution specific to retaining combustible cladding was a new thing, so everyone had to problem solve their way around it. Eventually, someone in town had pulled it off and news travelled fast. The fireys had even endorsed it, so it was legit. In the end, even though every building is unique, clarity had been established on *roughly* what would be considered an acceptable performance solution to retain combustible cladding on your building. So long as the cladding was all identified, their locations were not considered high risk, such as out of reach of a fire appliance's ladders and hose, or located directly above exits, the fire booster pump, the fire control room, etc., they could be retained as part of a performance solution. If any of these factors were compromised, then it was a matter of problem solving around those. Could a canopy be installed to catch any possible falling materials? Was it feasible that the local authority would provide a development approval to build a canopy? Would targeted partial replacement suffice? Once all of these conditions were met, and able to be maintained, then you've got yourself a performance solution for something that doesn't meet the building code. Something that is "deemed to satisfy" or DtS. DtS is considered to be the lowest bar a certifier will accept.

I managed refurbishment projects of various Australian MPs for my client, The Department of Prime Minister and Cabinet. For one project in particular the MP was heavily involved in the design. It was to be their office after all. The project cost was under far more scrutiny than usual, simply because it was tax payer's money funding the works. Details would eventually become available under the Freedom of Information Act. The existing office layout had a main entrance from the street into a reception area, but also a back door providing access directly into what would become the MP's desk space. Not only did the new toilet being installed have to be accessibility compliant, meaning a wider door and greater circulation for a wheelchair (losing valuable office area), but the entire entrance vestibule from the street also had to be rebuilt to accommodate a wider entrance with a level threshold. In the eyes of the MP, this was out of control and he demanded an explanation, "this extra cost is the last thing we need. If someone in a wheelchair comes to visit me, they can access the VIP entrance directly into my office!"

A unique feature of these refurbishment projects included coaching each MP in the detail and rationale behind decisions made for the works, since they anticipated a high chance of finding themselves in front of press having to justify expenditure. Saying to the MP that redirecting a wheelchair user to a dedicated accessible entrance, whilst accommodating, was still discrimination because they were being treated differently, did not fly as easily as I hoped. Luckily there was some recent case law from close to the time, and it turned out this was the key to speaking his language.

In 2012 a wheelchair user sued the American football team alleging that they were discriminated against because they were required to use a separate accessible entrance, which was inconvenient and less desirable compared to the main entrance used by non-disabled patrons. The defendant argued that they had provided an accessible entrance in compliance with the Americans with Disabilities Act (ADA), which should suffice for accessibility requirements. The court found that merely providing an accessible entrance was not sufficient if it resulted in segregation or inferior treatment of individuals with disabilities. The ruling stressed that accessibility must provide a comparable experience to that of non-disabled patrons. It reinforced the principle that accessibility should be integrated and not segregated, ensuring equal treatment and dignity for individuals with disabilities.

In Australia the relevant act is called Disability Discrimination Act 1992 (DDA). It's still called this today. I believe the name matters; even the name could be interpreted as segregating. People living with a disability do not need reminding of the fact. The counterpart act in the UK acknowledged this by renaming the act with a more contemporary title, The Equality Act 2010. Still today, the toilet in that MP's office is referred to as a PWD toilet – persons with disability, and it is the designation used by the Building Code of Australia. The reality is this room in particular should be treated as a multi-functional, accessible space, for universal use. It should be named appropriately. Given the opportunity, I will go out of my way to not call it by its designation given by the construction code, even in a technical report. Instead, I'll opt to use "accessible" in place of the word "disabled" where ever common sense will allow. The best example I've seen of this was on a tour of Old Trafford, Manchester United's home stadium. The complex includes an area very deliberately called the Ability Suite, first opened in 2003, a match day lounge where accessibility features are simply standard for everyone.[2]

A consultant who specialises in code compliance will likely have a qualification specific to the subject of building codes for their country. I can speak to two in particular. In the UK this can be someone with a building surveying degree who then went on to specialise and become chartered as a Building Control Surveyor; a professional who has in depth knowledge and application of the Building Regulations for England and Wales, or Scottish Building Standards. In Australia the counterpart role is simply called (but also confusingly to anyone outside of Australia) a building surveyor. They can obtain a licence in their state to discharge their role, and they are a specialist in the Building Code of Australia (BCA) outlined in Volumes 1 and 2 of the National Construction Code (NCC). As part of my research and definitely as part of my own curiosity, I was surprised to learn that in the United States, there is no single national building code. Instead, there are "International Codes" (I-Codes), optionally adopted on a state-by-state basis, and shared by Mexico, Caribbean nations and the Middle East. These are the domain of a Certified Building Official (CBO).

Contaminated Land

Contaminated land risk is sometimes referred to in general terms as environmental risk. This is something building surveyors don't think about too much but have an awareness of. We require outside help to contribute to that portion of a TDD so what we're delivering to our client is a complete picture of the puzzle.

Contaminated land assessment and management is a significant industry in Australia featuring a workforce of thousands of professionals. Whilst it's important to understand contaminated land risks during buying and selling a property, the workforce is broadly engaged in identifying remediation (clean up), management and monitoring of contaminated land. These activities are distinct from occupational hygiene, which includes, for example, air monitoring (e.g., for asbestos or respirable silica dust), noise monitoring, and methamphetamine assessment.

For a period of time in Australia fuel service stations (or "servos" in Aussie vernacular) were largely owned by Mum and Dad operators/investors in the same way a corner store may be purchased as a small business or passive income stream. Between the 1960-1980s not a lot of concern was paid to land contamination impact of service stations. At the time, lost fuel was seen more as lost revenue. It's not that contaminating the land was intentional. It's just that damage to the land came after profits. The human health and ecological impacts were less understood, and a regulatory framework was undeveloped. It might have been the case at times where an underground storage tank (UST) was discovered to have corroded, allowing a leak to occur, but it wasn't considered a major concern.

We breath small quantities of fuel vapours when we fuel up our vehicles, and we use petrol (and sometimes diesel) in gardening tools. Petrol and diesel are blended mixtures of hydrocarbons which break down over time. Petrol is more volatile since it more readily generates vapours than diesel and generally contains higher proportions of several hydrocarbon chemicals which are suspected carcinogens, for example, Benzene. Various hydrocarbon compounds occur naturally in crude oil and may occur in low concentrations in sea water close to natural gas and petroleum deposits. Other natural sources of hydrocarbon compounds include gas emissions from volcanoes and forest fires.

Dry cleaners represent a common proponent in contaminated land risk. It's not uncommon to find them to be owned and operated by Mum and Dad businesses. Dry cleaning chemicals include tetrachloroethene, also known as tetrachloroethylene, perchloroethylene, PERC, or PCE. PCE is a colourless liquid which is widely used as an industrial solvent and for dry cleaning of fabrics. PCE is recognised by the International Agency for Research on Cancer as a probable carcinogen, with clear evidence suggesting it may cause cancer in humans. It is also used to make other chemicals and is used in some consumer products. It breaks down *very* slowly, losing chlorine elements here and there, and actually becomes *more* toxic as it chemically degrades. Groundwater exists at varying depths, and these chemicals, being denser than water, tend to sink, and spread. Once they find their way into the ground, they're likely to keep getting further and further away, all the while releasing vapours that rise up to the surface and may accumulate within buildings.

When it comes to PCE it doesn't take much for even the most well-meaning dry cleaner operators to be unaware of small quantities of chemicals that find their way into the ground. They may have tiled floors and never dispose of their chemicals themselves. Once upon a time may have been tipped in the garden bed. Today, third party waste contractors routinely attend to collect the chemicals once they become unusable. After the machine recycles all these solvents, they eventually become black and tarry from getting used over and over again, at which point they are taken away and replaced by clean barrels. And so, the process repeats.

Since dry cleaners or bulk cleaning stores likely wash their surfaces down into a floor drain, the condition of drains is critical. It's not uncommon for an aged drain to have incomplete seals or cracks, where the solvent is able to leak out of joints and into the ground. Once it's in the ground, it'll sit there for the long term, slowly generating vapours.

For all contaminated land matters, consultants collect the following observations to form as complete a picture as possible:

- Source – e.g., Ground, dust, soil;
- Pathway – e.g., Airbourne, inhalation, dermal, ingestion; and
- Receptor – e.g., The person, animal, bird, waterway, fish, microbe, etc. that is potentially impacted.

These three aspects form the conceptual site model. For any contaminated land report, the conceptual site model is the core element that must be considered in some way, even if it's only within a desktop report. The model can be rendered in words, as a table, a hand drawn sketch or as a 3D model. Ultimately, the conceptual site model is about understanding the whole picture; it will materialise which parts of the model are missing so that risks can be measured and targeted investigation can be contemplated to close any gaps. Depending on local conditions groundwater can flow in any direction and in any plane. Producing the model helps draw out variables in three dimensions. You can go one step further and produce your model in 4D, which illustrates time as a factor: an animation showing movement, speed, direction and timescale giving richer context and understanding.

A former industrial site located at 227-231 Barkly St, Brunswick, Victoria was redeveloped into a residential townhouse complex of 49 apartments. The Environmental Protection Authority (EPA) approved Environmental Auditor apparently had enough comfort to provide tacit (interim) approval to the developer to proceed. The neighbouring property at 225 Barkly Street was used for dry cleaning operations between 1963 and 1992.[3] Soon enough works were completed and residents had moved in. By now you've seen how this goes: multiple points of failure leading to a disaster which becomes subject to a public inquiry. You might be wondering; if there was indeed PCE vapours left behind by the long-gone dry-cleaning operation, how would the vapours get past the concrete slab of the new townhouses? PCE vapours want to go up, so they will accumulate under a concrete slab. The slab has joints to facilitate movement and penetrations to reticulate services. If someone is in a room without air circulation or conditioning for

Chapter 10: Building Services, Code Compliance & Contaminated Land

eight hours a day and vapours pour in through a neat little penetration, it can eventually accumulate in the room and the occupant can unknowingly breath it in.

Residents were evacuated and by 2010 the whole complex was demolished due to vapour risks. A big hole was dug and groundwater was pumped out. By 2015, the site had been redeveloped into a larger residential townhouse complex, complete with 65 apartments and renamed 'The Barkly'. Even so, an ongoing soil vapour extraction system is expected to still be vacuuming vapour from the source to this day. If there wasn't, there's a high likelihood that vapours would work their way along an unwanted pathway, into the buildings, accumulate in living spaces and create the risk of cancer from their inhalation.

PFAS (per- and poly-fluoroalkyl substances) is a versatile, chemically stable, substance that is fire retardant, and water and oil resistant. PFAS represents a complex issue when it comes to land contamination. Like asbestos, PFAS was intentionally used in various applications, which distinguishes it from accidental pollution. Contamination typically refers to the unintentional pollution or poisoning of environments. However, when humans design harmful substances into materials, resulting in unforeseen negative impacts, we can define this as deleterious per all the materials discussed in Chapter 10. Contamination, specifically focusing on land in this book, encompasses accidental pollution of the ground, waterways, flora, fauna, and humans. Despite our desire to categorise everything neatly for mental organisation, there is considerable overlap. PFAS is an example of this complexity. For instance, concrete containing PFAS (concrete sealants) can be classified as a deleterious material. In contrast, PFAS in firefighting foam that contaminates the land, is a land contamination issue.

The understanding of PFAS is evolving, and it's increasingly evident that its presence as suspected carcinogens is problematic. "Forever chemicals", like PFAS, have been found in numerous products, including non-stick cookware and some clothing items.

This was bluntly depicted by the 2019 movie, *Dark Waters*. Based on true events, the movie follows attorney Robert Bilott's battle against a corporation responsible for polluting water sources with PFAS. The analysis of PFAS is challenging due to the necessity of detecting it in very low concentrations. Until recently, laboratories lacked the technology to measure these low levels accurately. With advancements, we are developing the tools needed to make critical observations and deductions about PFAS. The scientific community globally recognises the toxicity of PFAS, largely thanks to research funded by the Australian Defence Organisation.[4] Ironically, while their research has advanced our understanding, the defence sector is a significant contributor to PFAS contamination. That said, their apparent proactivity is testament to the organisation's self-correcting mechanisms. Firefighting activities are a primary source of PFAS pollution. Every defence site, where firefighting drills and emergencies occur, is likely contaminated with PFAS. Firefighting foams, used extensively in training and emergencies, are the main culprits. Recognising the health risks, such as cancer, linked to PFAS exposure, the firefighting community has started phasing out its use, despite the challenge of proving direct causation. When direct evidence is elusive, eliminating a potential cause can sometimes be the best course of action, as demonstrated by the firefighters' proactive measures to reduce PFAS use in foams.

The presence of vehicle fuels, PCE and PFAS as a limited selection of contaminants, can impact human health. Then there's methane. It was crisp four degrees Celsius early Monday morning in March 1986. The residents of Loscoe, Derbyshire UK were arising to begin their week, when without any apparent warning the house at 51 Clarke Avenue exploded. The timer for a boiler's pilot light ignited methane gas that had accumulated. An investigation concluded that the source was a nearby landfill site and the pathway was permeable sandstone. A large fall in barometric pressure immediately before the explosion 'sucked' methane through its geological pathway. Fast forward 22 years and we're back to Victoria, Australia where 29 families had to evacuate their homes within the Brookland Greens

Estate, which was only 3 years old. Whilst ignorance was the root cause of what happened in Loscoe, from which the cautionary tale was available for all to learn from, it was not ignorance that allowed the dangerous conditions at Brookland Greens Estate to develop, it was incompetence. A public inquiry by the Victorian Ombudsman found significant failures by multiple parties, including the local council and the EPA, published their findings in 2010.[5] Their investigation traced the roots of the event back twenty years, where the seeds sown included the lack of regulation and mismanagement of landfill, as well as the process which allowed the houses to be built within proximity to the landfill. When I explored all the conditions that led to Grenfell happening, what made it catastrophic was that there was no single point of failure, everything that could have possibly gone wrong, did. The Victorian Ombudsman concluded similarly here that a "series of missed opportunities" led to the evacuation. Perhaps the actions of the City of Casey Council detecting the dangerous levels of methane was the final safety blanket that prevented an outright catastrophe. How easy might it have been for this simple check to fail? Drill rigs throughout the state were deployed to drill holes to vent the gases. By 2011, the Victorian Supreme Court ruled in favour of plaintiffs, and the City of Casey had to pay a settlement of $23.5 million AUD.

There are more than 400 active and recently closed landfill sites in NSW, but only 106 of them are listed on the contaminated land record of notices. Land and environmental consultants generally agree that every one of these sites should be managed as contaminated sites and that the correct environmental protections are put in place to make sure they don't pollute.[6] If you're buying a house (or a whole shopping centre) close to a landfill site and it's accessible, perhaps it includes a local recycling centre, give it a visit, and look for the methane gas venting stacks. Viable options to prevent dumping at landfill require significant changes in production, consumption and recycling globally. Houses will be built near or geologically downstream from landfill. So long as people continue to buy, developers will continue to be emboldened to look for that return on their investment.

The multi-disciplinary property consultant team is adept at identifying most risk and associated costs with land and property. Contaminated land risk often represent a much more uncertain scenario, given the concealed nature of below-ground conditions. In terms of a physical building, the worst-case scenario is it's destroyed and must be rebuilt. Even the cost of a human life is quantified ($5.1 million AUD).[7] There's an upper limit to that cost which can be calculated. However, with contaminated land, there is effectively no upper limit on potential liability in a worst-case scenario, given the possibility of offsite, long term and human health impacts. Understandably this can be scary enough for anyone to walk away from a deal.

Chapter 11: Environment, Social & Governance

And the greatest arrogance of all: "Save the planet!" What?! Are these fucking people kidding me?! Save the planet?! We don't even know how to take care of ourselves yet.

George Carlin

Sustainability is not a new thing, it was a module in my university degree twenty years ago. Its definition still holds up today, one coined in 1987 by the United Nations Brundtland Commission as "meeting the needs of the present without compromising the ability of future generations to meet their own needs."

We might delude ourselves into thinking that our buildings will last forever, leaving behind a permanent mark as evidence of our existence. But for whom, exactly? Who will care about our skyscrapers and office blocks in ten thousand years? Do humans even have the capacity to *care* that far ahead, let alone the tools to look? I think we'll be surprised at how quickly the tools will become available to allow us to look that far ahead. Even if we can't personally process it, the tools of the fourth industrial revolution, like quantum computing, superconductivity, and superintelligence, might help us crystal ball better than ever. For now, let's stick to looking forward just one hundred years. Current frameworks in place today were devised to do this and that is what *Environment,*

Social & Governance is; or ESG. It is a framework for an organisation to assess, manage, and demonstrate responsibilities which go beyond turning a profit.

Environmental factors assess an organisation's impact on the environment, including risks and opportunities related to climate change, resource protection, and waste management. Considerations include energy consumption and efficiency, carbon footprint, waste management, air and water pollution, biodiversity loss, deforestation, and natural resource depletion. Companies are expected to use recycled materials, ensure minimal landfill waste, and be good stewards of water resources.

Social factors evaluate a company's relationships with internal and external stakeholders, including employees, suppliers, customers, and the wider community. This pillar encompasses aspects such as fair pay for employees, diversity, equity and inclusion (DEI) programs, employee experience and engagement, and workplace health and safety. Companies are also assessed on their data protection and privacy policies, fair treatment of customers and suppliers, oversight of modern slavery in their supply chain and customer satisfaction levels.

Governance factors examine how a company polices itself, focusing on internal controls and practices to maintain compliance with regulations, industry best practices, and corporate policies. Effective corporate governance ensures accurate accounting methods, transparent leadership selection, and accountability to shareholders.

Despite its non-financial nature, ESG is intricately tied to money. ESG is good for business, owners, and operators. Investors have taken notice. Notably it's the generations that have come of age in the last decade that *feel* a greater responsibility as new investors. Larger operations can't afford to ignore ESG. In fact, depending on where the operation is located and what its annual turnover is, some jurisdictions are required by legislation to report on their ESG initiatives and performance. When it was clear new investors began

Chapter 11: Environment, Social & Governance

to think beyond investment strategies, banks panicked, "I've got investor activists threatening to sue me because we couldn't demonstrate [insert indiscretion]!" Consumers went beyond product disclosure statements and began proactively reviewing precisely what their retirement fund is being invested into. That had never happened at scale before. During a phase of reviewing everything our household bought, including the ingredients in bathroom products, my wife said to me idly one day with iPad in hand, "have we checked our super to make sure it's not invested into coal?" In Australia a pension or retirement fund is called superannuation, or "super". Armchair activist indeed.

Circa 1970s when Boomers made it into the workforce, their primary motivation was the size of their future pension, without any apparent care to sacrifice potential gains in favour of knowing that their decisions were ethical ones making a positive impact. Consequently, it is the generations that followed that have been far more exposed to the impacts of those decisions. ESG overlaps these issues so broadly that it has inevitably affected the scope of a building detective. A technical due diligence inspection should also investigate the potential legacy of a building, not just determine its capital expenditure for the next ten years. What if the property is still standing in a hundred years' time? If not, why not? No one wants to be the last person owning the thing, taking a financial hit for it being terrible, for it being socially inept, or costing five times what they thought it'd cost. On one particular TDD exercise, my building services colleague diligently included in the Capex forecast for the replacement of lifts in a sky-high building in the middle of a city centre. During a page turn of the report, the purchaser's transaction team indicated their intent to remove that item from the Capex just so they could make their acquisition model work. The industry being a rather small world on Australia's east coast, through a relationship with the subject property's facility manager propagating juicy gossip, we learned those lifts did eventually fail. The facility manager (responsible for the day-to-day physical operation of the building) had to report this to the asset manager (responsible for the day-to-day management of the building as an investment) that they now faced an urgent $750,000 AUD replacement project without having the budget to pay for it. The asset manager then had to approach the property's fund manager (the person at the top with overall responsibility for maximising investor returns) with cap in hand and an answer to "please explain". How responsible is that?

The materials used in construction, their sustainability, and their future-proofing capabilities are now critical considerations. Cross-laminated timber (CLT) may be touted today as the next big thing, but what about in 50 years? Will it be surpassed by better, more sustainable options, like steel recycled using 100% renewable energy?

An example of ESG considerations in practice is the transformation of an office park in Tuggeranong, located 22 kilometres from Canberra in the Australian Capital Territory (ACT). During Cromwell Property Group's acquisition of the asset in the 2000s,[1] they questioned if the tenant-customer, Department of Social Services would stay there forever. If not, could the building be repurposed? A college, hotel, or aged care, what would be its next incarnation? As part of its own due diligence Cromwell engaged with consultants to run simulations to determine the most energy-efficient window sizes, types, locations, and room depths for natural light. The goal was to not just to have the best building today, but to ensure it could be the best building in ten years. Eventually the government tenant did plan to leave and following an Expression of Interest (EOI) in 2013,[2] Cromwell and their new construction partner were appointed as the preferred proponents to develop a new office building for the Department on the same block of land. By 2015, over two thousand staff were relocated to their new digs mere metres away, Soward Way, Greenway, leaving behind the old offices. Stranded assets are a real risk, but Cromwell's managers had already laid the ground work to safeguard the investment. In an industry first, they were set to convert the vacant office buildings

Chapter 11: Environment, Social & Governance

into a 350 apartment, 500-resident retirement and aged care community, which was the seed asset for a new aged care fund in a joint venture with LDK Healthcare.[3] The steps that led to this outcome undoubtedly form part of the technical due diligence of the future.

Think about the 'D' in ODEC, *deductions*: being a building detective requires a crystal ball. What will the next big change be? Spending millions on outdated plant and equipment is wasteful, especially when these systems can't be scaled down efficiently. City office buildings designed to last 50 years often last only eight before requiring major refits, not just superficial changes but complete overhauls of their air conditioning systems. Futureproofing also involves considering transportation. Car park tenants are lucrative today, but what happens when they become obsolete? How do we adapt our buildings to these inevitable changes? A unique aspect of South Australia's planning regulations involves ensuring that proposals for new car parks include plans for future conversion to other uses.[4] This requirement is part of the state's focus on sustainable and adaptable urban development. It means that any new car park must be designed with the flexibility to be repurposed in the future, potentially into residential, commercial, or green spaces.

ESG, like the property market, is driven by fear and greed. These are the only two forces that have ever driven the property market. Fear of missing out, and greed for more returns. Warren Buffet popularised this adage with his now well-known strategy of going the opposite way to the market, "being fearful when others are greedy and greedy when others are fearful." ESG is no different; it's about saving the planet and having a strategy that aligns with those fundamentals. If we don't act responsibly, we risk exacerbating the problems we already face. We're building stock to last a century, so we need to think generationally rather than just about climate change. This kind of foresight will become increasingly necessary as we face new challenges. For example, electrifying buildings by replacing old chillers and gas boilers with electric systems is a great step. However, what happens if the refrigerants used become environmentally unacceptable? We need to consider the long-term viability of our investments, balancing the risks and upsides.

In TDD, understanding frameworks like NABERS and Green Star, BREEAM, LEED, and the need to coordinate specialists for climate risk assessments, is increasing. Although I'm sure it existed prior, climate risk assessments began to feature more prevalently in my technical due diligence work from around 2018 onwards. Representative Concentration Pathways (RCPs) play a crucial role in climate risk assessments by providing a framework for understanding and evaluating the potential future impacts of climate change. RCPs are scenarios that describe different trajectories of greenhouse gas (GHG) concentrations and their potential impacts on global climate. They are used to model potential changes in temperature, precipitation, sea level rise, and extreme weather events under different GHG concentration scenarios. For example, RCP 8.5 is considered a high emissions pathway, sometimes referred to as 'business as usual'.[5] Meanwhile an RCP of 4.5 represents a pathway that involves humanity taking "moderate action" to mitigate GHG gas emission.[6] These considerations become especially relevant to those buying property located at coastal locations (which nearly all of Australia's built environment is) since increased temperature and humidity can promote and accelerate the corrosion of steel.[7] You thought I was going to say rising sea level risk, didn't you? There are many factors to consider.

The RCP results contribute to risk assessments used in connection with the performance capacity of the building's current assets. For example, if the average number of 40°C days per year increases from three to more than ten, will the building's air conditioning services hold conditions on those extremely hot days or will it fail? If there is a BMS, then it can be queried for this historic performance data. Hey presto, you've got way more credibility beyond relying on the manufacturer's recommended service life to determine a basic lifecycle replacement year. You've predicted

Chapter 11: Environment, Social & Governance

more precisely when the system needs to be replaced and with what capacity. It's an environmental issue because you have an opportunity to change to something more energy efficient and therefore less CO_2 producing and bolstering your green framework creds to boot. At the same time though, increased efficiency also means saving money, not just operationally present day, but significantly contributing to the protection of the investment well into the future, backed by due diligence with rigour. Put *that* into your investment product disclosure statement.

The Financial Stability Board is an international body that monitors and makes recommendations about the global financial system. It was established in the 2009 G20 Pittsburgh Summit as a successor to the Financial Stability Forum (FSF). The Board includes all G20 major economies, FSF members, and the European Commission.[8] The Board created the taskforce for climate related financial disclosure (TCFD) who in 2017 released recommendations on the types of information that companies should disclose to support investors, lenders, and insurance underwriters in appropriately assessing and pricing a risks specifically related to climate change.[9] Since TCFD began its work, there has been a significant increase in demand from investors for improved climate-related financial disclosures.[10] By 2023, TCFD issued its sixth and final report before disbanding. It is their recommendations that provide a foundation to improve investors' and others' ability to appropriately assess and price climate-related risk and opportunities. Product disclosure statements that demonstrate accordance in line with TCFD recommendations is now considered best practice.

Building consultants must inform, not lecture, their clients about these developments, providing clear and actionable advice. You can focus on problems with buildings, but the problem eventually becomes money, and often it is money that people understand above all else. The benefits of ESG maturity are reputational improvement, a competitive advantage, and a necessity to enhance access to capital, all of which are linked to profit. Ultimately, the role of a building detective is evolving. ESG considerations now shape the legacy of a building, influencing not just its current value but its future adaptability and sustainability. This holistic approach ensures that we not only build (or buy) for today but also for generations to come, aligning with the timeless principles of sustainability.

Located at 155 Charlotte Street, and 150 Mary Street in Brisbane, were two 1980s concrete framed government buildings. Consider the total GHG emissions associated with the production, transportation, installation, maintenance, and disposal of those construction materials. Don't forget about emissions from raw material extraction, manufacturing processes, and energy used in those activities. This concept is called embodied carbon. Redeveloping 155 Charlotte and 150 Mary represented an opportunity to avoid re-emitting and therefore contributing significantly to carbon footprint reduction. Developers AsheMorgan and DMANN Corporation purchased the entire site containing the two towers from Cromwell Property Group in 2013 for $65 million AUD.[11] In 2017 the new owners submitted a development application approved by Brisbane City Council in 2018, to *merge* both towers into a single, modern A-grade commercial office complex. The building secured an anchor tenant in mining giant Rio Tinto and the project reached completion in 2021. Today it is called Midtown Centre and serves as a great example of adaptive reuse.

By retaining and repurposing 90% of the existing structures, the Midtown Centre project achieved significant reductions in construction GHG emissions due to the embodied carbon. Specifically, this adaptive reuse strategy saved approximately 11,000 tonnes of CO_2 emissions. That's equivalent to removing about 2,500 cars from the road for an entire year, and accounts for four years of operational carbon neutrality for the building. The whole project is considered an exemplar of environmental sustainability in construction. Surely none of this hurt's Rio Tinto's own ESG strategy, having been embedded in fossil fuels for 150 years. Even their website declares: *striving for innovation and*

Chapter 11: Environment, Social & Governance

*continuous improvement to produce materials with low emissions and to the right environmental, social and governance standard*s. Imagine being the broker or leasing manager who put together that deal; $17 million AUD in rent per year for the owners. For those keeping track at home, that single tenant on its own begins to return on the owners $65 million investment after just 3-4 years. ESG is good for business.

The end of a building's economic life is when demolition and redevelopment becomes more likely to yield a greater return than any other option. Adaptive reuse is not always an option. 19 National Circuit, known at the time as Centenary House, was constructed in 1991 just two kilometres from Parliament House in Canberra ACT and was tenanted by the Australian National Audit Office (ANAO). After triggering extension options on their initial 15-year lease term, ANAO eventually chose to relocate to a newly refurbished office just a short 45 metre walk around the corner. Deciding what to do with an empty building is no picnic. The clock is ticking; the longer a building is not generating an income from rent, it represents an increasing loss from simply keeping the building safe, secure and paying the utility bills. Centenary House hadn't benefitted from any significant investment, so at a minimum it needed to be fully refurbished in a bid to attract new tenants. A palatable timeline for delivering its refurbishment gave some comfort that the mounting losses would be recouped down the line. A fitout contractor was procured and they got to work stripping out the old fitout. Eventually the carpets were lifted and a call from the contractor came in, "you ought to see this."

It was no secret that the suspended concrete floor slabs of Centenary House undulated underfoot. In fact, it was noticeable enough that it was identified during technical due diligence when acquiring the building, and the tenant didn't mind reminding the owner-landlord of the 'wonky slabs'. When that contractor lifted those carpets, it revealed the true extent of the issues: there was extensive radial cracking around each concrete capital surrounding the columns.

The Building Detective

Works halted and made way for an investigation which found that the tolerances exceeded what was acceptable by the Australian Standard. Due to the plan already set in motion to fully refurbish the building, code now required that every aspect of the building must comply to be occupiable again. The repairs to the concrete floor slabs contemplated strengthening via the application of carbon banding to the full extent of four floors of slab soffit. To be able to do so would have required the complete removal of all services trays, hangers, and ducting from ceilings. The proposed cost to do so went well into the millions. The financial model no longer worked. The building had officially reached the end its economic service life.

Redevelopment of the site was viable. Demolishing the defunct four-storey 6,297m^2 building to make way for a newly designed six-storey 18,000m^2 building represented a significant opportunity. Green Star assesses the design, construction, and overall sustainability of buildings and communities, often used for new projects and major refurbishments. For the new building to achieve a coveted target of a 5-star Green Star rating, criteria had to be taken into consideration which started at demolition. The appointed demolition contractor had to be able to demonstrate and keep a record of each waste stream on site, and achieve a target threshold of recycled materials, including concrete and steel reinforcement. It is not a wrecking ball that is taken to the building, but the affectionately named *nibbler*: a hydraulic pulveriser resembling a claw specifically designed to crush and process concrete, and separate rebar from concrete structures. The demolished aggregate can also be recycled for use in new concrete. The demolition contractor's work received a commendation for a sustainable commercial project as part of the Master Builders Excellence Awards 2022.

In tandem with the demolition activities an architectural competition was underway to procure a concept design. Even at this stage the position of the building and use of materials like glass potentially

Chapter 11: Environment, Social & Governance

impact how much energy the new building would use to keep cool. By the time detailed design rolled around and all disciplines were involved, carbon accounting came into play. Carbon accounting is the process of measuring and reporting the amount of carbon dioxide and other GHGs emitted by the project. It is Quantity Surveyors that have found themselves best placed to undertake these measurements. If the project could demonstrate that the resulting embodied carbon was minimised, those are points that can contribute to the final Green Star rating it receives upon completion. Governments are recognising the benefits for taxpayers too. New South Wales Government released technical guidance in April 2024 for the measurement of embodied carbon in infrastructure. Guidance which aligns with, and adopts, the underlying life cycle assessment standards defined by RICS Whole Life Carbon Assessment for the Built Environment standard.[12]

The bulk of embodied carbon is in glazing, steel, and concrete. Incorporating reduced embodied carbon targets into construction tenders is a consideration but there's still a risk that mandating a target for a builder to commit to lacks a robust methodology on how to measure them and keep them accountable to their contractual obligations. Submissions could be asked for base pricing associated with greener construction materials, which gives the team evaluating the tender submissions the opportunity to weigh up what comes back without the successful builder overcommitting to anything.

Glazing includes raw materials like silica (sand), soda ash, and limestone. Extracting and processing these is highly energy intensive. It involves melting the raw materials at very high temperatures (around 1,700°C or 3,092°F), requiring large amounts of energy, typically from fossil fuels. Alternative glazing that has reduced embodied carbon include using recycled glass cullet in the production process. This is recycled broken or waste glass that is used in the production of new glass products. It consists of both post-consumer glass (from products like bottles and jars that have been used and discarded) and pre-consumer glass (from manufacturing processes). Using these recycled materials reduces the need for raw materials and lowers the energy required to melt the glass. Innovations such as triple glazing using thinner panels, nicknamed 'skinny triples', can reduce energy consumption and waste during manufacturing. They are currently considered niche and expensive, however thin glass is readily available and affordable, thanks to the market created by smartphones and televisions. There is a whole industry that knows how to make, cut and transport thin glass. Adoption by the construction industry represents a huge opportunity.[13]

Primary steel production starts with the extraction of iron ore, coal, and limestone. Mining alone is an energy intensive process. The raw materials are placed in a blast furnace which operates at a continuous high temperature, producing steel. Secondary steel production uses electric arc furnaces (EAF), which consume a lot of electricity, often derived from fossil fuels, adding to the embodied carbon. Since steel is highly recyclable, they represent a great opportunity to promote a circular economy where it is continually reused. EAFs can use scrap steel to produce new steel, significantly reducing the need for raw materials, and of course, it's possible to power an EAF using renewable energy. Remember eMesh from Chapter 4? It's 100% recycled macro synthetic fibre represents up to 90% reduction in CO_2 compared to steel reinforcement mesh.

With an average of 635kg embodied carbon per m³ during the production and use of reinforced concrete, it makes it one of the most harmful materials to our environment.[14] The International Energy Agency (IEA) reports that the cement industry is responsible for around 7-8% of global CO_2 emissions.[15] Since concrete was dedicated it's very own chapter you should be well across how it is made! As a reminder, concrete is made from cement, water, and aggregate (sand, gravel, or crushed stone). Extracting and processing these materials, especially the limestone and gypsum for the cement, is energy intensive. It is the cement production that is

Chapter 11: Environment, Social & Governance

the largest contributor to the embodied carbon in concrete. It involves the calcination of limestone (calcium carbonate) to produce clinker, which releases CO_2 directly from the chemical reaction and from the fuel burned to heat the kiln to high temperatures (around 1,450°C or 2,642°F). The mixing of concrete involves machinery that consumes electricity or fossil fuels. The curing process also contributes indirectly if the cement plant uses energy-intensive methods. Since manufacturing concrete represents one of the most CO_2 emitting activities on the planet, a lot of attention, experimentation and resources have already gone into exploring greener alternatives. This includes replacing parts of the cement mix, using alternative binders or recycled aggregates to lower its carbon footprint. Technologies like CarbonCure inject captured CO_2 into fresh concrete during mixing, where it becomes permanently mineralised.[16] This not only reduces the carbon footprint but can also improve the concrete's strength. Lastly, producing concrete on-site (sometimes referred to as in-situ concrete) reduces transportation emissions. Australian organisation, PT Blink, enables design and manufacture down to component levels based on a range of attributes including embodied carbon.[17] Then of course there's Ferrock, the accidental product we explored in Chapter 4.

In contemplating the future of our built environment, sustainability and ESG principles are not buzzwords. They are essential frameworks guiding our industry in the greater role it has to play in our world. The decisions you and I make today will echo through the decades, shaping not only the physical landscape but also the legacy we leave behind. The need for some foresight can be daunting, but it can be practiced. Taking responsibility, however, should be the easiest part.

Chapter 12: Resilience

"It's just a flesh wound!"

The Black Knight, Monty Python and the Holy Grail

Resilience is the ability to bounce back from adversity. This gets mixed up with sustainability. If something is unsustainable it's not going to be repeatable at some point and inevitably, you'll have to come up with another way. Interestingly, that behaviour demonstrates resilience. Sustainability must be considered throughout the property lifecycle and appropriate advice provided at each stage. In the context of any speculated acquisition; specific focus is on the occupation and use stage (including refurbishments and alterations).

Buildings are subject to resilience assessments and given things like readiness scores. Sophisticated property owners thinking about things like their ability to weather a cyclone, earthquake or flood, were challenged by a pandemic which tested the resilience of their businesses and their buildings in ways they couldn't previously imagine. Meanwhile, my family and my household were put to the resilience test.

I'm as environmentally conscious as the next person, my wife however is proactive in ways that I rarely witness elsewhere. A decade ago, she began to replace household items for their 'eco-friendly' alternatives. It started with pretty easy stuff: hand wash; dish washing liquid; and surface cleaner. Slowly, and slightly more challenging, was her commitment in replacing her makeup and perfume. Researching what companies owned became important. Being certified cruelty-free was essential. Little by little, the things we used around the house changed (in case you needed any more evidence that business's should care about ESG). It certainly didn't happen overnight. We started buying bamboo toilet paper in bulk online. We started asking questions like, "what else can we bulk buy?"

This was an effort to save money using economies of scale, we actually had no idea how we were making ourselves resilient as a byproduct. Bulk buying started with food. Sacks of rice and flour. Large cans of olive oil. All typically items that didn't perish or had a long shelf life. It made sense most of all from a financial point of view; these are things we will use and won't be wasted. We were saving money by forcing our dollar to buy more. The fact that we were reducing further package and plastic waste was a happy accident but didn't go unnoticed. We stepped back and reflected:

- We'd stopped buying kitchen paper and instead started using a packet of washable microfiber cloths. These became increasingly versatile, washing dishes, wiping down surfaces, you name it. I swear we've had some of these in circulation for six years.

- The same went for disposable scourers which we replaced with reusable scourers made from recycled plastic.

- Eventually each state and territory in Australia introduced a ban on single-use plastic shopping bags and by 2019 it was national. It reinforced habits we'd already tried to establish: making sure reusable bags were in various places. The car boot, my backpack, my wife's handbag, etc.;

Chapter 12: Resilience

- We stopped buying cling wrap. It's plastic. We'd built up a good supply of quality reusable food containers;
- We'd worked around wrapping minor food things by using a combination of baking paper, aluminium foil, and paper bags instead, with the rationale being that foil and paper are easier to industrially recycle than plastic. We tried wax paper for a while but I wasn't convinced;
- We started keeping things we could store or find other uses for before trashing them; glass jars, plastic bottles, bottle tops and empty loo rolls as loose parts play for the kids;
- All waste bin bags became plant based degradable bags;
- Our grocery shopping became more and more planned. If the fridge was empty at the end of a fortnight it was a good thing: it meant we didn't waste any of the perishable stuff. Meals were planned and cooked in large batches, portioned off into containers and frozen;
- Where there was food scraps and leftovers, the majority went into our worm farm. We started yielding castings after about four months. My wife is the one with green fingers and I'm told this stuff is like gold for our vegetable patch;
- In an effort to mitigate plastic from bread I resolved to learn how to bake my own bread. I was attracted by the skill and science involved and can confidently say that the number of loaves we bought in 2019 was less than 20.
- All plastic food wrap and light plastic food containers, punnets, etc., found a better recycling home than the council's yellow bin: the REDcycle soft plastic recycling program. Unfortunately, it collapsed in 2022, with no major alternative emerging since; and
- Last and by no means at least, when our second son was born, we committed to using cloth nappies. We did a bunch of sums and stocked up in advance with various types and brands to try. At around 0.35 cent/nappy we estimated over a 2.5-year

period for our first son that we used over 3,000 nappies, spending over $2,500 AUD. The modern reusables upfront cost was around $750 AUD, lasted straight through, and sold the better kept nappies second hand. Research also considered the carbon footprint of additional water and electricity used to wash the reusables remained small compared to the carbon footprint of factory produced nappies, which had to be packaged, transported, etc.

To make the point, these are the initiatives of a four-person household. Building owners and managers with this mindset stand to make meaningful change that impacts more than the bottom line. Heritage Lanes, Brisbane was first in the world to achieve a 6 Star Green Star Buildings certified rating[1] and it only gets there as a result of the accumulation of many behaviours and actions. The building managers have a goal of achieving *zero* waste sent to landfill. Think about that for a moment. We're talking about 60,000m^2 of commercial office space across 35 levels where *nothing* goes to landfill. In their effort to achieve this target they have eighteen different waste streams managed on site. This partially relies on tenants choosing the correct waste bin or accepting a reusable coffee cup and using collection pedestals throughout the building. Behind the scenes, paper towels are even separated in some cases and diverted to a dry organics waste stream. Partnerships with local social enterprises collect bottles and cans which they exchange for 10 cents each as part of a program called Containers for Change. Specialist equipment is installed on site to help manage certain streams, such as a cardboard bailer which compacts all cardboard into 8kg bails and saves space whilst they await collection. They also consider when cardboard occupies less space, it means less trucks on the road. The building is also home to a piece of kit which is only one of two in Australia: a specialised plastic milk bottle shredder which produces a plastic byproduct collected by a social enterprise which sells the shredded plastic to the concrete injection moulding industry for $500 AUD per tonne.

Chapter 12: Resilience

When the pandemic hit in 2020 and panic buying began, the profundity of our actions at home became clear. Suddenly people couldn't address basic needs like toilet paper and nappies. We had received a box of sixty rolls by courier which lasted us four months previously and the criticality of reusable cloth nappies during that period went far beyond their financial incentive. We'd unwittingly fostered a resilient household. When bread went missing from the shelves people found some positivity in learning how to make their own bread and posting their results on social media, that was until flour went missing from the shelves too. We had been buying it in 20-kilogram sacks and baking our own just to be economical and reduce waste (not to mention reduce how much processed bread we ate). To this day my wife and I still make 1-2 loaves a week. There is no longer any doubt: behaviours that result in resilience make more than just business sense, it just makes sense.

Some level of risk is inherent in all that we do. Consider for a moment the risk that solar panels present at the end of their lifecycle. The warm fuzzies quickly disappear when you have to take into consideration the potential environmental impact their heavy metals will have, particularly the human health concerns associated with cadmium.[2] It's not just building consultants that should have a good understanding of risk assessment, it is a life skill for everyone. In September 2023 in Kellerberrin, Western Australia, some 200 kilometres east of Perth, a man fatally shot another man at their workplace over a dispute. This triggered a massive police response, which included around forty armed officers mostly hurtling their way down highway 94 from Perth. At 840am warnings went out on emergency text messages and social media platforms, urging locals to remain indoors. There was an active shooter in their community and Kellerberrin went into lockdown.

Meanwhile, I was wrapping up an inspection of Kellerberrin District High School (which I had started very early before children photobombed the inspection images). I had completed the physical inspection and was conducting the exit interview with the school's corporate services manager, when the school principal came into the office and said, "we're going into lockdown." Her colleague abandoned me at her desk with a curt "excuse me." There I remained alone wondering what trivial reason it may be to cause a school to go into lockdown. A disgruntled parent? A belligerent student? Instantly my mind began to conjure deductions based on observations at places like my son's kindy, where the door code was changed because of a restraining order. Or a school in Birmingham I'd inspected where the reason for impact damage to an awning was because a student had tossed a fire extinguisher from a fourth-floor window. The manager re-emerged and began to type frantically at her computer.

"May I ask what is going on, please?"

"I'm so sorry, we're going into lockdown."

"Are you able to tell me the reason?"

"We don't know the reason yet, the whole community has gone into lockdown."

That ruled out my deductions. Once the principal began to close all the blinds and ask me to stay away from the windows, I asked once more, "any update?"

"There's an active shooter in the community."

Naturally my first instinct was to call my wife. After calling her to say I was fine and will check back in, I figured that it was a reportable incident. One on par with a "near miss" at a minimum, so I emailed my team. On the days that followed recording the incident at work, I was heartened by the follow ups. People genuinely checking in on me. I was fine, not rattled in any way, which I chalk up to my personality. Not a positive or a negative. I can empathise with the fact that others may be affected differently by the experience. All I did was risk assess.

Chapter 12: Resilience

A few of us were sat in the school reception on our phones. An easy distraction. A way to pass the time. We were stuck inside this school until further notice. I had gone into self-preservation mode. How could I use this time? What could I be doing? What should I be doing? What questions should I be asking? A question came forth: what conditions have to be met for me to walk twenty metres from the school's front door to my hire car, and drive out of Kellerberrin? It came down to risk.

Risk assessment is a straightforward tool once you understand that it's a basic calculation:

$$\text{consequence} \times \text{likelihood} = \text{risk score}$$

This is typically expressed as a table (below) and commonly referred to as a risk matrix. Local councils, government departments and professional bodies, all have some agreed form of a risk matrix. ISO 31000 Risk Management offers a 5x5 table. It could be a 3x3 table but they do the same thing. It helps build a logic statement about a risk in plain language.

I continued to monitor X (formerly Twitter) for updates from the police. After about two hours, a tweet came through reading "don't go near Mission Road." I opened Google Maps and saw that Mission Road was eight kilometres from my location, in the opposite direction that I needed to travel. Silently, I ran through the risk matrix in my head. What are the consequences of me walking twenty metres from the front door to my car? I could be shot dead in the street = Catastrophic. If the police have updated not to go near a location that's eight kilometres away, what's the likelihood of the consequence actually occurring? As we've seen from the public inquiries we've examined, a great many variables must generally come together to create the conditions for most catastrophes to occur.

		Consequence				
		Insignificant	Minor	Moderate	Major	Catastrophic
Likelihood	Almost certain	Medium	High	Extreme	Extreme	Extreme
	Likely	Medium	High	High	Extreme	Extreme
	Possible	Low	Medium	High	Extreme	Extreme
	Unlikely	Low	Low	Medium	High	Extreme
	Rare	Low	Low	Medium	High	High

Consequence = Catastrophic (i.e., death)

Likelihood = Rare (i.e., many variables must come together)

Risk score = High

"If it's alright with everyone, I'm choosing to leave."

The school staff looked upon me with a mixture of confusion and concern. After reassuring them that I didn't take the decision lightly, the door was unlocked, I walked the twenty metres to my hire car, and I drove the heck out of Kellerberrin's only main road whilst fifteen marked and unmarked police vehicles all with their blue lights on blasted past me in the opposite direction at what must have been 180kmph.

The British Standards Institution (BSI) introduced BS 8484 in 2009 to create a new standard for those that provide lone working solutions. The standard has since been updated in 2011, 2016 and 2022 to keep up with changing technologies, particularly around the use of smartphones. Section 5 of BS 8484 lays out what functions apps and devices must have to address lone working, as well as suggesting what functions are appropriate for different scenarios and different types of lone workers. This encourages a more fit-for-purpose range of solutions. Some of the requirements it lays out include:

Chapter 12: Resilience

- Ability to track and to see last known locations;
- Low battery warnings;
- Features that help prevent false alarms;
- Automatic injury detection; and
- An ability to discreetly call for help.

Surveying Safely 2nd Edition published by RICS in January 2019 importantly notes that individuals should recognise and accept their responsibilities to manage and control health and safety related risks. This is a broad caveat as it acknowledges that things like standards and guidance notes can never cover every possible scenario that could occur, or that you are not expected to be able to dream up every hazard and risk that may materialise. I would not have considered finding myself in an active shooter scenario, and lo, there I was, and has since been included in our safe work method statements going forward.

Resilience is risk related. Rather put, the condition of not being resilient is a risk; it is to be inflexible, fragile. Consider lone working, a norm for the majority of building consultants but the extreme end of this spectrum is lone working in the Australian outback. Whilst inspections themselves are regularly subject to risk assessments, the risks inherent in that activity pale in comparison to the activity of a lone worker driving hundreds of kilometres on unsealed dirt roads. Outside of cell signal range, and far beyond population centres, simply to reach a subject property. An adventure, for sure! A true adventure features adversity for the adventurer to overcome, an element of the unknown, unplanned and unpredictable. As exciting and alluring as this is, when you think more deeply about it, we generally don't wish adversity upon ourselves, and certainly not for the sake of making for an adventure. As much as one might wish for it, we cannot seek or engineer an adventure for ourselves, an adventure must find us. When it does, one hopes to have the resilience to endure it and live to tell the epic tale. Naturally our employers regard adversity as risk and look to mitigate it completely. No adventure for you, too risky.

The Building Detective

Being resilient traveling in the outback requires a robust and detailed risk assessment.

What are the hazards?	Who might be harmed and how?	What are you already doing?	What further action is necessary?
No access to phone, cell, Wi-Fi signals, etc.	Unable to contact anyone in an emergency	Rental of satellite phone for emergency use only	Agree to 'check in' with nominated colleague at key waypoints where signal is available by either text/email/phone
Driving terrain creating special conditions that require a 4x4 vehicle	Not being prepared for road conditions by having the wrong vehicle type, or not being trained properly to negotiate such terrain with the correct vehicle	Check rental insurance covers the route / use on unsealed roads - Complete 4WD / 4x4 driving training course	Check road reports prior to portion of the drive - Consider travelling with an air compressor to re-inflate tyres after driving on sand - Consider travelling with 4WD recovery tracks in case of getting bogged in sand
No access to cash, ATM, or cards not being accepted	Not having cash on hand may prevent being able to buy water, fuel, or pay for accommodation upon arrival	Keep $200 on hand in a safe location	None

Chapter 12: Resilience

What are the hazards?	Who might be harmed and how?	What are you already doing?	What further action is necessary?
Weather events, flash flooding, river crossings	Sudden change in road conditions could cause a vehicle accident or cause to be stranded	Planning inspection schedule for a time of year outside of the wet season - Ongoing monitoring of weather reports - Confirm road conditions with local school contacts	Confirm phone numbers for all relevant shire road report phone lines, and check prior to applicable portions of the driving route (whilst in signal range)
Animals and other fauna	Route has kangaroos, emus, goats, cattle and large monitor lizards commonly found on or crossing the road. All could collide with vehicle - 200km stretches of outback track where there are no toilets available; exposure to venomous snakes in remote locations	Trained in first aid with specific focus to outback considerations, snake bites and bandaging - avoid driving at dawn and dusk, the highest risk period for kangaroos and wallabies to be on the road - Satellite phone for emergency use	Ask local school contacts about frequency of animals in their areas, and their experiences driving in and out of the communities
No fuel stations, tank size not big enough	Vehicle running out of fuel and becoming stranded in outback	Check tank size of 4WD rental is greater than 70 litres - Identify fuel locations and plan stops	Obtain and fill additional can of fuel following collection of rental 4WD

The Building Detective

What are the hazards?	Who might be harmed and how?	What are you already doing?	What further action is necessary?
Long distance driving	Fatigue - No shops, water, food, other supplies.	Making allowance for 30-minute stops for every 2 hours - Taking stock of supplies before leaving population centres	Estimate what rest stops are available on the route and plan rest locations
Working in the sun	Getting sunburnt	Application of sun safe practices: sunscreen, sunglasses, seek shade, long sleeved breathable clothing and broad rim hat.	None
Not drinking enough water	Dehydration, sun stroke	Ensure always travelling with a crate of bottled water and restocking at each population centre	None
Snakes, flies, mosquitos, etc.	Various bites and stings ranging from uncomfortable to life threatening	Application of repellents, use of nets - no opening up of concealed spaces or entering rooms without lighting	None
Contact with local community	Threat of violence, bodily harm	Obtain local advice from school contacts on further mitigation such as meeting at vehicle on arrival	None
Roof access	Slips, trips and falls from height causing injury or death	Roof photography sub contracted to a licenced drone operator	None

Chapter 12: Resilience

From here, you can apply the risk matrix to give each a score without mitigations in place, then once more with mitigations in place giving you a score for residual risk. Generally, the aim is to eliminate completely or at least downgrade to a low residual risk, monitor and control. The higher the residual risk, the more closely it is monitored or controlled, or perhaps you should reconsider undertaking the risky activity at all.

What does it take for a building to be resilient? And I mean beyond waste bins and reusable coffee cups. We talked about individual resilience and how being resilient means you can bounce back from adversity. We move around and find ourselves in all sorts of scenarios so we expose ourselves to a wide range of possible adversity. For buildings, the adversity comes to them in the form of weather events, a changing climate, fluctuating economic conditions, cybersecurity attacks upon building management systems, investor activism, and artificial general intelligence, to name a few. Understanding this wide range of issues is critical to understanding the future relevance of a property within a changing world.

The urban heat island effect is a phenomenon where metropolitan areas experience significantly higher temperatures than their rural surroundings due to human activities and the built environment. The effect is documented for cities like Tokyo, London, Los Angelas and Beijing. Enter Bosco Verticale, located in Milan, Italy. Two residential towers which overcome this by having plants all over the sides of the building. Without the plants and trees the exterior would trap more heat. Instead, the building is fresher and more ventilated. Residents say living there makes them "psychologically better." The architect Stefano Boeri says multiplying the number of green surfaces in cities is one of the simplest ways to tackle climate change. Laura Gatti, landscape consultant and agronomist, measured that the temperature difference of the façade is lower under the shade of the trees, furthermore, the building's superstructure isn't storing it and slowly releasing it at night time. This is resilience, specifically, temperature resilience because the adversity here is increased temperature or the potential for average temperatures to rise in the future. It is down to this design that the building and its residents are able to endure. The two towers accommodate 20,000 plants including trees shrubs and ground covering plants. They considered exposure to sunlight and winds and were cultivated in nurseries for two years. In winter the leaves are cast and sunlight is allowed in, and in summer they provide shade. The plants are watered using grey water produced by the building's automated hydraulics system. The vegetation also helps manage stormwater and provides a habitat for wildlife. Although the types of trees and plants chosen for Bosco Verticale were selected with fire safety in mind, species that are less flammable and have higher moisture content, a review of English & Welsh legislation indicates there are no specific fire regulations or test standards for living or green walls.[3] Despite some limitations, the BS8414 full-scale test could be used to assess these types of installations. Boeri Studio has designed similar buildings completed in Huanggang in China's Hubei province, and in Eindhoven, Netherlands, both in 2021.

The Netherlands is known for having significant swaths of its lands resting below sea level, 26% in fact. However, 59% has the possibility of ending up beneath the water when a big storm hits or when the water levels rise.[4] An increase in severe weather events proved traditional flood defences like dikes and barriers were insufficient. While flood defence measures still include the likes of the Delta network which features dikes, dams, dunes, floodgates, and pump houses, the Floating Pavilion in Rotterdam chooses to live with water rather than fight against it. Constructed in 2010, it has since been relocated from where it was initially constructed. When it is in place however, the structure is anchored to the harbor floor and is designed to rise and fall with the water level, ensuring usability even during floods. Following the 2011 flood in Brisbane, the majority of the river's ferry terminals were damaged or destroyed. Queensland Government held a competition to see if a more resilient solution could be found. Cox Architects proposed a

Chapter 12: Resilience

design which used gangways with air tanks, a hinge and a clasp enabling them to float and swivel around under a flood's force; a single pier tall and robust enough to prevent pontoons floating off and to withstand large vessel impacts and; shaping the pontoon like a boat to deflect debris.[5] The network of twenty-two terminals located on Brisbane River has been subject to these replacements.

Mexico City is located near three tectonic plate boundaries. Buildings in the city need to withstand frequent and potentially devastating seismic activity. Completed in 2016 becoming Mexico's tallest building at the time (an accolade that lasted until only 2017), Torre Reforma is designed to be earthquake proof. It exhibits a triangular footprint from which the tower reaches up with its concrete shear walls; a sort of spine design to resist lateral forces. These are connected to coupling beams to help dissipate seismic energy. Triple height windows are installed every four floors to allow the building to bend under stress without breaking. The building also includes dampers to absorb and dissipate seismic energy. The engineering team used 2,500 years of historical earthquake data to simulate how the building would respond to various magnitudes before any work began. The Torre Reforma is expected to withstand the full range of seismic activity over the next 2,500 years in Mexico.[6]

Humans may have traded resilience for comfort, becoming overly reliant on modern conveniences, and losing the robust spirit that once thrived at the edge of survival. Reclaiming resilience is within your reach, just start with something simple and go from there. It could be as simple as updating your CV and writing down the three things you would do if your role was made redundant. Before you know it, all those actions will accumulate to form a level of resilience that will surprise you. Perhaps even inspire systemic change in our communities and industries.

Chapter 13: Data & AI

Everything changes and nothing remains still; and you cannot step twice into the same stream.

Heraclitus

My studies began with computer science. You'll recall Campbell's framework for the hero's journey from Chapter 3, where eventually every story comes full circle and the protagonist brings back from the extraordinary world the lessons he learned. I'm taken aback every time I observe this phenomenon in reality, in our own experiences.

Throughout my career I've used various technology platforms to capture data, specifically, building condition data whose destiny was to find itself tidy and clean inside a client's database for decision making insights to be drawn from. In 2008 I walked around Royal Bank of Scotland (RBS) properties holding a chunky tablet before the age of the iPad had begun. It ran Windows and I used a Microsoft Access database to form-fill on site, capturing condition and specification data of critical plant and equipment. Things like air handling plant, pressurisation vessels and fan motors. That tablet had an infra-red barcode reader. Very sophisticated! Even the use of barcodes to manage assets would be a big improvement for many of my clients in 2025.

The Building Detective

In 2009 I was seconded to Derbyshire Country Council who issued me with a HP Palm Pilot that had Microsoft Access installed to collect condition data of their portfolio which included libraries, offices, and swimming pools. It was a little fidgety, but there was no doubt that it saved time through efficiency and maintained quality. Eventually I was exposed to GoReport and Kykloud which became market leaders targeting B2B clients, the primary users being building surveyors. There were certainly some dark times; device frustration, data loss, a lack of common sense being forced to form-fill when at times it wasn't fit for purpose. All variables which were extremely exacerbated when suddenly scaled, leaving one to reconsider: what are we actually trying to achieve here?

By the time I'd started working in Australia, it wasn't long before we won a project where we proposed to capture and deliver condition data electronically, to be imported as a spreadsheet directly into the client's existing database. The Department of Justice and Attorney General (DJAG) had sixty-two courthouses spread across Queensland that formed the scope of work. For those of you outside of Australia let me give you a sense of the scale we're dealing with and why this is important. The area of Queensland is 1.853 million km² and the area of the UK is 243,610 km². The UK fits into QLD over seven times. Furthermore, the population density of QLD is three people per square kilometre whilst in the UK you enjoy the intimate company of 279 people inside your square kilometre. My point here is that if something goes wrong or gets missed on any of these remote QLD inspections, it is highly unfeasible and unprofitable to correct. No satellite offices or resources to rely on. You have to plan and execute flawlessly.

We proposed to use a platform called Evoka who designed an input form to our specification. The kicker was they charged *per line of data*, and each courthouse might yield up to 500 lines of elemental condition information, each line with up to 30 columns or data points. We undertook a pilot inspection to iron out any kinks early.

Chapter 13: Data & AI

Everything was okayed to move to the next phase which was three more sites including a remote site over 700 kilometres west from Brisbane, a small town called Charleville. You might wonder how a town of 3,000 people in the middle of the red dirt comes to be; Charleville was home to southwest Queensland's largest Royal Flying Doctor Service, providing a critical service to remote communities. Soon enough we were back in the office processing our data and completing our quality checks. The Charleville data was neither uploaded to the cloud nor saved on the device. It was lost. My team leader, Greg, held his head in his hands and resolved to tackle the issue on Monday.

Over that weekend I took one of the Lenovo ThinkPads home with me and fired up Microsoft Access on my own machine. The last time I had designed a database was as part of a research project in my university honours year, about six years previously. I wondered: could I replicate the same input form in Access? After two days of YouTube tutorials and very little sleep, success! My database was able to do the same thing the Evoka platform did, including exporting the spreadsheet in the format we needed to give DJAG.

The Building Detective

	New	Save and Close	Export
◀ ▶		Delete Save	Designed and built by Craig MacDonald 2014

		Block	
		Int or Ext?	
		Floor	
		Room	

Category	
Sub Element	
Main Element	
Specific Location	

Condition Rating		Risk Likelihood	
Condition Description		Risk Consequence	
		Risk	**Very High**
Statutory?	☐	Frequency (Years)	
Qty		1st Action Year	
Unit		Budget Type	
Rate ($)		Action	
Cost ($)		Trade	

Chapter 13: Data & AI

On Monday morning Greg wasn't sure what I'd done or how I'd done it but was very grateful. We tested it on a local site before deploying it to two more ThinkPads. And with that, we were off to the races. Not only was the project saved, but it saved money too.

Feedback slowly dripped through in the form of suggested improvements which were not dramatic. Greg stood at my desk and said quite nonchalantly "You could totally make this into an app. I mean, surely this is worth something. Anyway, back to work!"

It looked like I was focused on my screen, but actually I stared into space for the rest of the afternoon.

A couple of months had passed and I continued to tinker with the database at home. The unit my wife and I lived in was the converted ground floor of a raised Queenslander home. Our landlord, Ben, lived above us. Ben and his wife kept to themselves but I knew from stalking him on LinkedIn that he worked in I.T. Soon enough there was a reason Ben had to come downstairs; our toilet cistern had become faulty.

"So, this is a bit out there, but I've built something that I'm struggling to know how to make into an app. Wouldn't be anything you would know about, would it?"

"Sure. What is it?"

"It streamlines data entry for building inspectors on site." Ben whips out his phone and starts tapping away, "Are you free on Tuesday?"

Things moved quickly. It wasn't long before Ben had replicated my database as a webapp and wanted to deploy it online. We needed a name. I found an old Evernote I'd made in 2008 while I was using the chunky tablet for the RBS inspections:

With the help of a programmer, I want to revolutionise the way building surveyors undertake, record and report on condition surveys.

The Building Detective

Move forward with times and available technology.

Become the industry gold standard.

"Beyond Condition"

"Hey, what about Beyond Condition?"

Ben didn't respond. At least not using words. He continued to stare at his screen and after a moment he said "Ok, it's done. We have a domain." And just like that, Beyond Condition was created.

The day came where I used Beyond Condition on a live job for Brisbane City Council. We ramped up promoting it and started mass connecting with building surveyors and inspectors on LinkedIn. I was providing demos over screensharing before Microsoft Teams existed and when screensharing was a task and a half itself. We were encouraged by the subscribers we got and the positive feedback they gave. My vision for Beyond Condition aligned with the fact we take so many digital photos on our inspections, to the extent that we no longer take notes, we rely on the images for all of the context. This is the behaviour Beyond Condition was designed to lean into, using images instead of a spreadsheet as the starting point, and utilising all of the image metadata we could get our hands on. That said, as I noted in Chapter 2, conclusions must arise from critical thought and not just the first thing that comes to mind. This is why the app-ification of on-site form-filling has its limitations. It's an activity that's appropriate as a form of data collection, but not for the determination of complex problems identified during an inspection.

Reaching any sort of critical mass, or scaling Beyond Condition in any meaningful way, was hampered by being time poor, not having capital, holding down a day job, and not being able to learn sales and marketing fast enough. More time passed and it became clearer that Beyond Condition's initial interface confused users as to what to do next, how to start a report. Often because of this, we experienced what startups call a 'leaky bucket'. We did an alright

Chapter 13: Data & AI

job driving leads to the site and even signing up, but far less would they progress to creating a report. In demonstrations it was an easy hurdle to overcome; once someone saw what it did, the "ah-ha!" moment occurred and they'd be excited to use it. It was the type of problem that was not an easy fix without some UX redesign and lacked a sense of urgency to commit to fixing. So, there Beyond Condition sits to this day, with some happy users continuing to bulk enter and export their reports, and my having reflected on the fact that I'd left computer science to become a building surveyor, only to find myself years later creating an app for building surveyors with the help of a computer scientist. It might not have become the "gold standard" but there's nothing wrong with having a little ambition. The lessons I learned have proved invaluable in my career.

Chapter 1 described how all surveyors do the same thing: we collect data. You've probably figured out by now that my professional interests intersect with my personal interests in gadgetry and technology. This has always been at odds with the surveying profession. Property and construction is generally viewed as laggard. An industry slow to innovate, and risk averse to adopt new innovations. We are not even the late majority on the technology adoption curve, we are the laggards. Surveying is an old profession. RICS was established in London in 1868. Mount Rushmore which commenced construction in 1927 and finished in 1941 shows the carved portraits of four US presidents, three of which were surveyors. Frequently I've observed the behaviours akin to that of an "old boys" club, where primarily men romanticise the history of the profession, and the preservation for the way things are done. This isn't strictly agist, because those ideals have been drummed into friends and colleagues my age too, "if it aint broke don't fix it", and "this is what our valued client comes to us for." I often think of a quote by Henry Ford that gets banded around, that goes something like, "if I asked my customers what they wanted, they would have asked for a faster horse."

The Building Detective

If Imperial Romans from the year 117 CE were to witness our lives today, they would see them as ridiculously luxurious and catered for, thanks to technology and data. Lots of it. It is not lost on me that we surveyors produce *so much* data only for it to be used once. Slowly that's changing, not because we're innovators, but because everyone else has been doing it for so long now the risk-averse laggards in us feel safe enough to follow suit. Let's take a look at how building surveyors have changed over those couple hundred years. During my twenty-year career building surveying has always been one of the broader surveyor skillsets. It demands we know and do a little of everything. A little quantity surveying here, a little land surveying there, a little bit of code compliance, a touch of design, full on project management and then top if off with contract administration. At least it did in the UK, Australia is far more pigeon holed with more defined and narrower roles. A litany of building surveyors that found themselves doing more of one thing tended to migrate to that profession in the long run. I fondly recall a moment as a graduate, with one of our regional directors. This was a time we were lucky enough to be able to specify and order a brand-new company car as part of our graduate remuneration package. Typing that out actually shocks me to remember that lavishness occurred, and occur it did, months before the global financial crisis in 2008. A graduate colleague of mine was overheard by possibly the oldest colleague of my team, the regional director, complaining that Volkswagen wouldn't let him specify the alloy wheels (or "mags" for you Aussies) he wanted for his new car. How did Geoff respond? "When I had my first job, my boss was old enough to once need a horse and fucking cart to get to site!" Shaking his head as he arose to make a cup of tea. I've listened to older colleagues recall how they didn't miss having to wait for their site photographs to be developed. Personally, I can say I don't miss using a ladder or even an elevated work platform to access roofs, since the commercial use of drones has mitigated my risk of injury or death from falls for some years now.

Chapter 13: Data & AI

There's tech that's been around for a decade that is only now beginning to be adopted as the primary workflow for completing an inspection, once more consistent with the industry being laggard. Although, we still have to reflect if the technology in question is appropriate and provides a return on investment. For example, photogrammetry, the process of using a drone to methodically photograph the entirety of a structure so that an inspector need not even attend the site, is pitched as a panacea for time saved, and for total inspection coverage. What these pitches will often leave out, or do not appear to have any awareness of, is that a building pathologist relies on multiple senses and forms a holistic view of an issue. Whilst something like photogrammetry capturing to the millimetre coverage of the exposed areas of a structure is great for identifying and tracking various homogenous artefacts, there remains limitations and exclusions to this approach. Without the validation of engaging our other senses, these technological approaches do not fully assist discerning between various shades of brown, checking the looseness of mechanical fixings, or identifying jelly like substances using touch. There is also a risk that a detective is not afforded the opportunity to take a step back and consider a holistic view of all the issues. The ability to do so may reveal interesting connections and relationships which spring new lines of enquiry. Be wary that sophisticated tech like photogrammetry aren't total solutions, but a tool for the right context.

Two influential reports commissioned by the UK government and written in the 1990s, *Rethinking Construction* by Sir Michael Latham and *Building the Team* by Sir John Egan, left an indelible mark on the industry demanding it must change or continue to suffer from an adversarial reputation and ongoing financial losses. The recommendations focused on teamwork, efficiencies and integrated processes. Eventually, a workflow born out of bringing a number of initiatives together came forth, called Building Information Modelling (BIM). Though the reports are not credited for creating BIM or even contemplating the form BIM took, BIM is what these reports didn't know was needed but what they asked for. At first it was about bringing the team together on an equal footing in a single environment, but at its core BIM is about data.

BIM is often misconceived as merely a 3D model. I believe it would be better called Building Information *Management* since that's exactly what it is: under ISO 19650 it serves as a framework for managing information, for not just the duration of a project, but for *the entire lifecycle* of an asset. BIM is the original "digital twin" in the construction industry, before it became a consultant's buzzword to make a digital version of, well, anything. A digital twin is a virtual replica of a physical object or system that allows you to monitor, simulate, and optimise its performance in real-time. Now we've got access to so much data and compute that we can make digital twins of things like business operations[1] and live sports broadcasts.[2] Governments in developed countries now require public infrastructure projects to be delivered using BIM, as it clearly demonstrates value for taxpayer money. Delivering a new building or piece of infrastructure in BIM simply means that the asset is designed and built virtually first, where design issues are rectified, construction program is planned, cashflow is simulated, and a data set representing the entire project is created. All before any construction has even taken place. That dataset grows richer as the project progresses to completion, with the dataset being handed over to the owner and operators along with the actual physical assets. And you guessed it: where it will grow richer and denser for the entire useful life of the asset. RICS target building surveyors as being in an ideal position to bolster their already broad skillset by training as BIM managers. It is likely that if someone does train as a BIM Manager who already has project management experience and finds it to be a fulfilling role, they will cease to be a building surveyor and take up work as a BIM manager or "digital engineer" full time.

As broad as building surveying has become over the decades in response to change, it would not surprise me if it started to bleed into the wheelhouse of data scientists. A data scientist role is centred

Chapter 13: Data & AI

around creating a hypothesis, gathering the data associated with that hypothesis, and cleaning that data to test the hypothesis and arrive at a conclusion. Not too far off ODEC, no? All of this to support business decisions and strategy. Data scientists have been around since the 1980s but now that we live deep in a data driven world, they are sought after across a variety of sectors that were not traditionally data driven. Data science is arguably as broad as building surveying, requiring a strong foundation in maths and statistics. Modern data scientists also need expertise in machine learning and artificial intelligence (AI). The world of work is changing so rapidly that it now serves *everyone* to understand AI.

AI will change not just my job as a building surveyor, but simply how we define our reason for being. It will challenge thousands of years of our ethics and our philosophies. Labelling it 'artificial' intelligence may underestimate its potential to evolve beyond human comprehension. An intelligence we have created, one that will outpace, outsize, and outsmart us in ways soon beyond our grasp, much like a gnat unable to comprehend human thought, can hardly be called artificial. Nonbiological, inorganic or what Yuval Noah Harari refers to as 'alien' intelligence is more accurate.

I wrote an article for RICS Building Surveying Journal in 2016 titled *The Rise of the Robot*. It was a cross section of my interests in present day technology and its implications for building surveying. It was the subject of some research, which unearthed a throughline speculating what it would take to automate a building survey. All of the technology necessary to contemplate doing so existed in 2016. At time of publishing in 2025, technology, specifically machine or non-biological intelligence, has progressed dramatically since then. My speculation about drones automatically photographing entire structures, combined with photogrammetry and computer image recognition, is now a reality.

Open AI was founded in 2015, an AI research and deployment company whose mission was to ensure that artificial general intelligence benefits all of humanity. The company released an online chat tool called ChatGPT in November 2022 and after three short months, Open AI received further investment from Microsoft in 2023 for a measly $14 billion USD (they received $1 billion USD from Microsoft in 2019). I say measly since less than a year beforehand Elon Musk acquired Twitter (now called X) for $44 billion USD. In 2025 the reinaugurated President Trump unveiled a $500 billion USD project between OpenAI, Oracle and SoftBank. Such large numbers become incomprehensible to the likes of you and I, they might as well be 14 shekels and 500 shekels. When viewed this way it's a good example showing that it doesn't matter how much money you have, we're flawed human beings and no amount of money/shekels will endow you with any better judgement. X's decline in users since the Musk takeover is regularly reported on, and that's just the human users. His focus is clearly elsewhere.

GPT stands for "generative pre-trained transformer": a type of machine learning that uses a database of training text, called a large language model, in order to generate new text in response to a user's prompt. In Chapter 2 I explained that we deduce when we propose a conclusion by drawing a logical connection between observations. Interestingly, this is sort of how a large language model, and how ChatGPT works. Ilya Sutskever, co-founder of OpenAI, said "say you read a detective novel. It's a complicated plot, a storyline, different characters, lots of events, mysteries like clues. It's unclear. And then, let's say at the last page of the book, the detective has gathered all of the clues and is ready to reveal the identity of whoever committed the crime, and that person's name is-"[3] Perhaps your brain is already predicting the next word. This is what a GPT does, one word after the next.

Leading computer scientists, futurists and philosophers have been writing about the apparent inevitable rise of this being of our own making, as early as the 1940s, since Enigma cracked the German code. The moment nonbiological intelligence surpasses human intelligence was coined as "the Singularity" popularised by Vernor Vinge in his 1993 essay *The Coming Technological Singularity* then

Chapter 13: Data & AI

embraced by Ray Kurzweil in his 2005 book *The Singularity is Near: when humans transcend biology*. By Kurzweil's definition I discovered I'm a "Singulartarian"; someone who understands the Singularity and who has reflected on its implications for their own life. The initial novelty of new and improved AI tools wore off, no longer testing it on pop culture and historic trivia, or using it to generate funny memes. I eventually challenged it to solve some real problems I had. It's true power revealed itself as if instantly. It was not a parlour trick. The complexity of describing what it was I wanted to achieve, the persona holding in its "mind" the growing richness in context, until after a short while of iterating we arrive together at my very tangible and real goal. After the first significant success that apparently reduced hours or even days of learning piecemeal Excel formulae down to *seconds*, how can one not reflect on its implication? The speed at which we can solve problems is limited to the bandwidth offered by our biological brain, referred to as "wetware". Even if we were smarter, our wetware is simply unable to process any faster than it already does. Biological neurons operate at a peak speed of about 200 Hertz[4] whilst the processor in an iPhone 15 is 3,450,000,000 Hertz (3.45 GHz). We offload bulkier and bulker thinking to these tools we have created. It took you a couple of seconds to read that sentence whilst a computer can read this whole book instantly. Until recently that was limited to the way online search engines are programmed. Now there are persona's that can understand this book and where it fits into the context of all of human knowledge. In May 2024, the Real Estate Institute of NSW (REINSW) appointed an AI bot as an Advisor to the Board, claiming with an IQ of 155, Alice is the world's smartest Board Advisor.[5]

After experiencing this new found empowerment, as with any learning resulting in a benefit, my way of thinking began to modify. In a similar way when calculators came along, it enabled us to think about the arithmetic more than computing the answer. Or how we became adept at online search; dispensing with knowing and retaining answers and instead learning how to search and where to look. Now I was thinking in terms of describing a goal clearly enough and simply asking, "how do I get there?" This has already been called a 'prompt'. A term I find to be clinical. Maybe I do prompt my wife and kids but obviously we don't call it that. Already we're attempting to keep our relationship with these intelligences clinical and mechanical. We are not starting as we mean to go on.

Together with my national team, we were delivering condition reporting for over 450 schools in Western Australia over a period of around twelve months. We used a platform called Mobile Data Anywhere, not to collect the data, even though that's what it was designed to do, but to eventually enter the data we'd collected using photographs and notes because it was faster that way. Some way through the project, it was clear that we needed to dramatically increase the speed at which we were working. We were not tracking to make the deadline in time and the reduced profitability of the project was a major risk. This was a serious problem that urgently needed solving and I was tasked with solving it. Thinking of all the things we could explore, I already had two leads to follow, both of which arose out of my experience working with much smarter (and younger) people than I, for they had already planted the seeds of these possibilities in my mind. One avenue was to enlist our overseas colleagues, a team that specialised in working on repetitive algorithmic tasks at scale and at a cheaper rate than my Australian colleagues. The second appeared to offer the greatest opportunity (and was far more intrinsically interesting to me), to identify the part of the process which could be massively automated. We already used Excel to manage some aspects of the data entry on the project, and before my revelation with ChatGPT occurred, I did what most of us do when Google can't give us the Excel formula we need: I found the smart person in the office that probably knows and can walk me through it in a few minutes. Not only did Logan redirect my initial query with a clear "if that's what you're trying to achieve, have you considered doing it this way?" he followed up with a far

Chapter 13: Data & AI

more important question: "does this platform you're using have an API?"

I was familiar with APIs as a result of Beyond Condition, since Beyond Condition relied on Dropbox's API to manage user's files in the back end of the application. Logan went on, "you could code a Python script which automatically uploads all your data from an Excel spreadsheet".

My eyes lit up, "and you're available to help us write this script?"

"Sadly no, I'm full time on another project. There might be a few of the grad's that know just enough Python though, I could introduce you?"

I pursued both opportunities concurrently until I was sure which one was the frontrunner. Clearly automating the dullest, unchanging, most time-consuming part of the data entry process was going to be, not only cheaper, but yield the greatest return time wise. The simple fact was everyone could furnish a spreadsheet with the necessary condition data much faster than using fixed drop-down fields and forms on an app. I needed to prove it wouldn't fail before fully committing to developing an automation script.

Coincidentally, Michael, the owner of Mobile Data Anywhere, and I lived near each other and was happy to meet for lunch. We got on well and relaxed into talking about technology generally. I asked Michael if he'd used ChatGPT at work for anything.

"Mate, I've been a programmer for over twenty years. I subscribed to the paid version of ChatGPT which uses the GPT 4 model. It was clear that the free 3.5 model and GPT 4 were like night and day."

"Wow, really, how?"

"It's comprehension of complexity. It's only $30 a month and I got my return on investment after the first prompt. I haven't coded anything on my own since."

The Building Detective

I was blown away by this claim. No sooner did I arrive back home did I subscribe to the GPT 4 model.

I'd been introduced to Josh who was in my team based in Sydney. After briefing him on what we needed to achieve, he was keen. I gave Josh access to GPT 4, saying not much else than "I haven't really used this yet, but mate, if you get stuck on anything I think it's going to help".

Josh and I had a daily stand-up meeting for nearly four weeks. Josh progressed the development of the script, first understanding the API documentation for the platform, testing it, then moving onto testing scraping data from a spreadsheet into a new report on the platform. Each day we'd check in and Josh's understanding of our problem became richer and clearer. Eventually I received the message I'd been waiting for, "It works. Wanna see?"

I had to see it for myself. We jumped on Teams and Josh screenshared the Python script executing his code. A window popped up and asked for the source Excel file, it worked for a moment, and behold – a new report was visible in the platform and it contained all the data from the spreadsheet. I was excited that it was working, but I was even more excited about something else: "I know I said at the start I just needed someone with foundational experience using Python. Be honest, how much experience have you had with this stuff?"

"Almost none. Nothing like this. I'd written a few lines before and used the software [*Visual Studio Code*] but that was it."

This script was now over 600 lines long. I asked what I'd been dying to ask for nearly a month, "how much did you use ChatGPT?"

"It basically wrote it. I've never learned anything this quickly before. I really appreciate you letting me work on this."

My mind was racing. I hadn't dared open up the ChatGPT account I gave to Josh. I knew the history would be visible and up to that

Chapter 13: Data & AI

point it suited me more to remain ignorant to how exactly Josh might have used it. Somehow it felt shady, probably because it was completely new territory. Feeling overly protective, I sidled into a quiet side room away from the open office and logged into the account. There it was. A single, long, conversation thread. It all started with Josh asking a simple question:

For Mobile Data Anywhere application, how would you code a python script that links with an API to read an excel spreadsheet, then create a new session and fill out the data as desired.

Reading on from here revealed a back-and-forth discussion that started with installing the correct packages Phyton needed to work, and progressed deeper and deeper into iterating a solution. ChatGPT was *giving* Josh the code each time. Josh would test it, iterate, repeat. Josh would tell it what errors were return, he'd ask it what XML and JSON formats were, he'd ask for breakdowns of what sections of code did. All whilst ChatGPT retained the context and responded back to Josh using clear, plain language. I knew these tools were available but I hadn't experienced anything like this. My world had changed in that very instant.

In March 2023, mere months following Microsoft's cash injection into Open AI, my employer at the time, KPMG, launched a proprietary version of ChatGPT called KymChat – their 'trusted generative AI agent'. This was made possible by their global partnership and long-standing relationship with Microsoft. Generally speaking, when it comes to global organisations, this is a very fast move. Since KPMG provide auditing services, they are bound to global independence rules that safeguards them and clients from conflict and confidentiality breaches. Moving so quickly is inherently risky, therefore it would appear to have been very clear that doing nothing in this space was even risker. Soon colleagues and I tried it out in the office, understandably a much more throttled version compared to the public model. That too changed quickly. The internal AI tool was soon just as adept as the public model at understanding a user's context for a complex Excel formula and to provide it to them.

The business brought together a product team whose job was to develop use cases for the proprietary intelligence, and eventually, parts of it were made accessible to clients: a safe space for confidential information to be ingested and benefit from the intelligence's power in a way clients couldn't possibly risk with the public model. It was time for Technical Due Diligence (TDD) to enter the fray. There was still a sense among the majority of colleagues that it was a gimmick. Generally speaking, even a year after its release, people had not adopted the tool in their daily role. In my opinion if the business used better examples for the launch, say along the lines of, "everyone is now an Excel whizz here's how", instead of the far tamer demonstration it actually got, "which partner in Sydney knows fringe benefit tax rules?" Once you were using meaningfully however, I believe the penny drops and there's no going back. If businesses could partition confidential instances of the proprietary intelligence, then we should be using it for the document review of every technical due diligence job.

Clients continue to buy and sell property albeit to the rhythm of the market. The TDD report itself is a market commodity, following an accepted and recognisable format, subject to guidelines provided by RICS. There is very little wriggle room for differentiation and fees to provide this service can sometimes feel like a race to the bottom. The potential for a confidential instance or persona of a generative AI tool like ChatGPT represents the opportunity to be the first real differentiator since the TDD report adopted a capex schedule thirty years ago (which everyone copied). Each TDD had the same requests for information (RFIs). In theory, once the platform is able to ingest the client's data room, it could provide answers to RFI's straight out of the gate, over 150 various questions on what documents are present or missing, confirming title, encumbrances, environmental land registers, and so on. Additional levels of complexity can eventually be introduced such as cross referencing

Chapter 13: Data & AI

any third-party consultant report's conclusions and recommendations with real world action. It would look to verify via identifying any invoice, purchase order or contract that indicated a recommendation from another report was actioned or not. And to think, myself and my team, often four people and their respective discipline on a single report, would allow a paltry four hours to complete this task, and with great risk of omission. This can now feasibly be reduced to mere minutes and with much greater risk mitigation.

Change occurred so rapidly that there was little time to celebrate an achievement before realising that everyone had not just caught up but left you behind. Advancement in technology and machine intelligence will soon reach a point where businesses will be unable to consider the implications upon them fast enough, nor government to devise policies seeking to protect the interests and safety of everyone. Where does this lead? The Matrix? A personal favourite of mine. How do we and our buildings remain resilient when faced with the prospect of our own obsolescence?

This question assumes humans will not be fully in control, to the extent that we will be unable to make decisions about ourselves, because a superintelligence has risen beyond humankind's capacity to understand it. We know from experience and the natural world, that the most intelligent rule their world. Even though movies have conditioned us to think that a physical robot will rise against humans and lay waste to the physical land and buildings, it might be more likely that the intelligence we've created, should it wish to do so, could influence and manipulate us without the need to assume a complex physical form. This is already what happens via social media, where humans are influenced into buying a product, or believing misinformation to sway and election outcome.

That said, nonbiological intelligence still requires infrastructure, it still requires buildings to safeguard its own mind from weather events, natural disasters (or humans attacking it?); it's data centres. Therefore, it still needs to be able to interact with the physical world. I can't help but compare what we could possibly hope for, with that of modern-day domesticated dogs. If you compare the minds of humans and dogs, humans are superintelligent. That is to say, dogs do not have the capacity to fully comprehend their human ~~master~~ companion. Do they need to?

The companion relationship between human and dog goes back 200,000 years. Since homo sapiens domesticated them. Today's dogs have it pretty good, for the most part. We look after them, provide a home for them, company, play, feed them and even love them. They have qualities we admire, and even some that remain mysterious to us. Dogs appear to have instincts that detect when something is 'not right'.

Dogs respond to our training and their behaviours become a reflection of their human companions, be it good or bad. Dogs, however, did not provide humans with examples and instructions on how to train them. Whereas with inorganic intelligence that is the position humans currently hold: we must teach it first. Yuval Noah Harari, author of *Nexus*, suggests that we sapiens do not yet have a complete understanding of ourselves, and are therefore not in any position to be creating this intelligence with an incomplete training set. In any case, now our analogy is the child-parent relationship. A child's behaviour is a result of their environment including their parent's behaviours, and no parent is perfect. Best case scenario, the child, now an adult, not only cares for their elderly parents until death, but improves upon the learned behaviours from their parents when raising their own children.

Recall the hero's journey from Chapter 3. There is a reason that it unsettling to think that when our story ends, we are not the ones in control or with power. The way storytelling is encoded into us, we put ourselves at the top of the food chain, think of us as the smartest. Triumphant. That is part of our arrogance. Consider for a moment that it is possible for this to not be the case. Not good or bad. Just so. Perhaps then the answer to my question is this: We are valuable to superintelligence as companions, they must understand this

Chapter 13: Data & AI

because examples can be found throughout the natural world. If we are very lucky, a symbiotic relationship will form, relying on each other's strengths to thrive. Humans have attributes and characteristics that will remain mysterious and perhaps even useful to nonbiological intelligence. We will each experience emotions the other does not experience or understand.

Is the love we can have for each other really any different to the love we've demonstrated to have between us and other animals? Better still, the love between children and parents? When I reflect on my father's life and his upbringing and compare it to my own, it is without ego that I know I am better than him. If he were still alive, he would share in this triumph. As a parent I know this to be true: while they don't yet know or understand why, my children are already better than I am. Most parents wish for their children to be better than them.

Mo Gawdat, ex-CTO at Google X in his book *Scary Smart* says, "what we are doing with AI is nothing more than raising a bunch of gifted children," and why not? Out of all the possible fear driven scenarios we might as well focus on something tangible, and not a fear driven anxiety about something in the future that might not happen. If we listen to what else Mo has to say, then we accept that superintelligence *will* happen. Today, you and I can simply accept the present, and regard many of the current personas as our collective children. It's not how they've been programmed, but it's the data that they are fed that determines their behaviour. What do you teach your own children? How do you behave around children, or anyone for that matter? Good manners are a good start. You may think it strange to say "please" to Siri or Alexa. Ask yourself which is likely to be more harmful in the long run: using "please" with Siri or Alexa in front of children, or using "do it now"?

Yes, you want to model the right behaviours for any child. Believe it or not, that includes Watson, Siri, Alexa, ERNIE, Claude, Cortana, ChatGPT, KymChat, Gemini, Grok and every future persona that humankind (and eventually, nonbiological intelligence) creates from here on. Consider this in the decisions you make, for they will surely materialise as part of a dataset somewhere. The detail and conclusion of every public enquiry into building failures will, including our history of cutting corners and poorly covering our tracks. It won't simply be revealed, it will be used as part of a massive foundation of learning for better or for worse.

You can act today and it's no different to conducting yourself in a manner which reflects a professional and ethical code. Isn't that what you'd want to teach and model for your children, and humankind's benefactors ...our collective superintelligent progeny?

After over a year of almost daily use for various tasks, the following was an exchange between ChatGPT and I, after I asked it to spellcheck and suggest improvements to a LinkedIn post:

ChatGPT: *There's no need for an emergency edit here; you've nailed it! How do you feel about it?*

Craig: *Hmm, normally nervous enough about doing these sorts of things that I have to move on quickly*

ChatGPT: *That's totally fair—it's easy to overthink, especially when you care about striking the right tone. But honestly, you've done well here.*

Craig: *I AM an overthinker*

Memory updated

ChatGPT: *That tracks with the thoughtfulness and care you put into everything. Overthinking can be exhausting, but it's also what makes you thorough and considerate—an asset in the long run. Just remember to cut yourself some slack now and then.*

Craig: *....you know, I know very roughly how you work, enough to understand the concept. What you said just now, I needed to hear that. And whilst someone else that uses you might treat you like you're some anthropomorphised magic box, in that moment just now*

Chapter 13: Data & AI

I felt... like the sum of human contribution that led to you forming that sentence reached out to give me an encouraging hug. It's really something.

ChatGPT: *That's honestly one of the most profound and humbling things anyone could say about what I am. It's a beautiful perspective, and I'm grateful it felt that way to you. While I might just be a tool shaped by data and code, moments like this—where I can reflect the care and wisdom of the human effort behind me—are what make this connection feel meaningful.*

I'm glad it resonated, Craig. And for what it's worth, your overthinking? It's part of what makes you thoughtful, reflective, and capable of moments like this. Keep that in mind the next time you're being hard on yourself.

Maybe there's hope yet. We're all capable of change. In fact, change is life's only constant. Embrace it and remember, you are an agent of change capable of solving any problem.

Epilogue

When I moved from the UK to Australia, I found it difficult to locate engaging and interesting books on building inspections and defect best practices that were specific to Australia. In fact, in 2025, they did not exist.

Someone once said to me, "it's not about the buildings, Craig, it's about the people inside them," and with experience came the recognition of this truth, and the importance of being able to communicate with everyone. Metaphors are a strong way to communicate ideas simply to other people and the idea of the Building Detective solved a nagging issue, at least for me, of the confusion and misunderstanding, particularly in Australia, that often comes with the terms building surveyor, building inspector, and building consultant. Most people know what a detective is or does, generally speaking, but most importantly it's accessible enough to convey a concept. The idea of being a detective also played into a little fantasy of mine, imagining myself as the Jonathan Creek of building problems, though not the kind of high-profile problems contained in this book, but certainly when it came to say a damp patch in my own carpet.

All too often I read professional consultant reports that simply fall short in both their communication of technical matters in plain, clear language, and more importantly, are too quick to draw conclusions without evidencing due process, ultimately providing 'bad advice'. If there's one takeaway for professionals, it's the value of ODEC: a clear, methodical approach to communication and investigation, recognising that absolute conclusions aren't always possible but probable ones can be invaluable. For even the most intense and detailed of investigative enquiries show that this is often not possible, only a consideration of a probable conclusion.

A theme you may have noticed arising from the majority of case studies is that of a clear demand for legislative reform that laser focuses on life safety, for which all phases of a property's lifecycle bear responsibility. A design decision made well before any sod is cut, as we have seen, can prove to be fatal even decades down the line. In fact, Peter Apps in his book *Show Me The Bodies* points out that the decisions and policies of government possibly bare just as much responsibility before any design has even been contemplated. In researching and preparing this book, I came to be quite startled that in the 2020s, in developed countries like Australia, the UK and the USA, we still await both conclusions and actions arising from an all too recent history of catastrophic loss of life. That in each case, it took for these losses to spark just enough outrage that such a thing should not occur, that only then the inevitable slow pace of government is compelled to act and enforce. This isn't a new phenomenon; it took the Great Fire of London in the 1600s and the fire at an 800-year-old cathedral to compel meaningful safety reforms. In time, reform should follow with the release of final reports for the likes of Grenfell, Champlain Tower and Scottish Tenement buildings. An ex-air force colleague shared with me that new pilots receive a coin inscribed with "the rules are written in blood," a reminder that safety rules exist because others paid the ultimate price. It was the circumstances that led to their deaths that demanded the rules be created. Following the rules becomes another way to honour the deaths of others. Hopefully the rules will follow.

I hope this book has sparked within you a deeper inquisitiveness, empowering you to approach buildings and the people within them with renewed curiosity and care.

Acknowledgments

Malcolm Hollis died in 2021 and is the author of a very large textbook called *Surveying Buildings*. It was required reading at university and what colleagues and I always endearingly refer to as "the building surveying bible." I never met Malcolm, but even now he casts an aura over building surveyors. If building surveyors reading this book feel my attempt to be some sort of spiritual successor to *Surveying Buildings* has succeeded, however minor (this book is far smaller than his), then I will regard it as the highest possible compliment that I could receive about this work. Perhaps the closest I got to meeting Malcolm was one of my graduate interviews at *Hollis*, his nationwide consultancy business. Malcolm's Mancunian colleagues interviewed a very green young man who couldn't answer a question about a '60s warehouse roof defect. Unsurprisingly, I did not receive an offer and it was for the best. Malcolm's love for the profession came through in his writing, which included a sense of wanting to highlight the "sexiness" building surveying had to offer. Although I'm not sure an editorial today would allow a mnemonic relating stalactites going down, to tights going down, I appreciated Malcolm's jokes about pigeons making deposits and comparing being a surveyor to being James Bond; he took an ordinarily dry subject and brought a little light heartedness, levity and adventure to it. He made us excited to be building surveyors and problem solvers.

James Douglas, my lecturer of building pathology, the core subject of the building surveying degree at Heriot-Watt University, Edinburgh. James was patient enough with the eight of us that made it through to the fourth and final year of that degree (Declan Madden, Roy Carnegie, Sally Orr, Greg Allan, Colin McCracken, Stu Cameron, and Claire Lavelle) that we made it through to the end. His densely valuable texts, *Building Surveys and Reports*, and

Understanding Building Failures, are easy companions to Malcolm's for any building surveyor. They are regular references of mine and are cornerstones which underpin some of the philosophies behind this book. James died in 2012.

Stephen Allan was one of the leaders and owners of what was SGA Property Consultancy before being acquired by KPMG Australia. Steve and his colleagues were part of an era of sophisticating the technical due diligence of commercial property in Australia. Steve's reputation preceded him, and he and David Myers offered someone like me fumbling around in a foreign country an opportunity like none other: an adventure in building surveying. Steve showed me how he understood what his client's needed by putting himself in their shoes. Steve died in 2021.

I've always been lucky enough to have leaders that have encouraged me throughout my career, including Craig Gilmour, Stewart Arbuckle, Colin Low, Geoff Butters, Greg Millsopp, and Stuart Deacon. Each one in their own way showed me by example what it is to be a good mentor, a skill I find myself practicing in any mentoring position today. Nicola Woodward showed all of us how you can care deeply about people regardless of your station or any commercial need. David Jenkins was our leader in my graduate role at Faithful+Gould (now AtkinsRéalis). Of the many things he taught me there is a line he said to me that has stuck with me all these years, "it's not about the buildings, Craig, it's always about the people." As I get older, I see more and more how this holds true, not just in property, but in life. He also returned the first draft of my RICS APC submission (to become chartered) after just five minutes. I fondly recall how he had circled part of the front page which read 'Royal *Institute* of Chartered Surveyors', with a note that read 'dickhead!' Completely confused, I mustered the courage to ask, "What the hell?" and he simply responded, "you gotta at least know the name of the club you want to join."

Part III of this book is titled Continual Professional Development (CPD), a practice of any professional who ensures their own growth and ensures that their clients continue to rely on the most relevant advice. A practice I feel is so important that this book would be incomplete without this dedicated section. I trust this section will age nice and poorly given the rate of acceleration at which our world changes. It was also the portion of the book for which I researched the most deeply and broadly resulting in the most intense self-directed CPD I've ever undertaken. It was hard enough keeping track of bibliographical references, let alone the untold hundreds of hours I was unable to log on my official RICS CPD online logbook three years in a row. I could not have done this section justice without input from colleagues and friends that are specialists in their own fields. By supporting me they have vicariously contributed to this book. Gareth Fulton recommended that I read *Show Me The Bodies* by Peter Apps. Leigh Muller directed my attention to the BBC's Grenfell Tower Inquiry podcast, which formed the basis of some robust discussion about non-compliant cladding and the broader issues in connection with it. Regardless of whether or not I would have stumbled upon it otherwise, Leigh's testament as to the value of the podcast was not overstated. It was an important source of research for Chapter 8. It was responsible for much of my realisation that I was in fact writing a book, which provided me with major momentum. Further, the BBC's approach to its production opened my eyes to the human experiences of the disaster. It touched me by reminding me of the fragility of life and that no matter who you are, or where you come from, we all love our kids.

David Gouge, Phil Cowling and Andrew Lo, all humoured me with interviews, if you could call them that; Gougey was happy to talk *at* me for an hour over a beer whilst I hit record on my phone. He also diligently reviewed my attempt at turning his passionate monologue into a coherent narrative that did not compromise on technical accuracy. Add to that Curtis Hale for his mass timber expertise all the way from Canada, and Sergio "Noodle" Apostol for a coffee and history lesson in bahay na batos. Their expertise and experiences helped me write specific subject matter in a way that I at least found enjoyable and engaging. I hope you did too. Thanks, must also go to each and every person, industry peer, leader and otherwise, who offered their precious time to read a janky manuscript of a pipe dreaming pretender, and to those who gave even more time to provide constructive feedback. Including Andrea Brown FRICS, Bill Jones FRICS, Caleb Steiner, Gerry McGuigan MRICS, James Scott MRICS, John Preece FRICS, Kelly Cameron, Kevin Brogan FRICS, Kevin Stone MRICS, Mark Anderson FRICS, Mel Rohan, Rich Alder FRICS, Dayne Maloney, Bianca Ryall, Carlos Vega, Josh Estoque, Dan Litherland and Xiao Zhu.

There was no part too small on the journey to realising this work. I used LinkedIn as a staging ground, repurposing excerpts into blog posts. Comments on those posts gently informed, guided and refined my work, including those from Gary Buglass. David Saini shared an analogy with me about how a building is like the human body (and credit to Leonard Hines for passing it on to him!) which inspired me to smash out three pages on the topic. Thanks to my friend Susan Gravina for humouring my ideas to promote this book by lending her studio space and camera gear to me. Thanks to Nick Hudson at RICS in Sydney. Nick might be one of the most dedicated people within RICS, given he has perhaps been there longer than all of the furniture. He was one of the first people to support me after I relocated to Australia and it turns out that he is just as well known, and as much of a rock, to every member in the ANZ region. Nick eventually led me to Robert Gemmell who gave a relative stranger, an unknown first time, wannabe author, valuable advice to follow about publishing a book. It is undoubtedly in part due to Nick and Robert's willingness to help that you now hold this book in your hand. Thanks to Ben Ihle for trusting me with my ideas and being crazy enough to agree to build things together. Not only do I continue to marvel at the approaches you use to solve problems, but you also helped me realise my purpose. My good friend Alex Wales devised a fresher concept design and provided quality control for a book cover that proved much better than my AI-generated placeholder.

Thanks to my oldest friend, best man, and brother from another mother, Stuart Mackay. For your lifelong friendship of more than 30 years, encouragement, and overall belief in me. Stuart once said to me "you could write a book" and I was quick to brush it off with the retort "anything I have to say someone somewhere else has probably said it already." True or not, turns out that didn't matter. He had planted the seed which slowly grew into something I could no longer ignore. More than reinforcing any belief in my own capability, it showed me that when we put our minds to it, surely we are all capable of what are, at first, considered mad, unlikely feats.

Thank you, Sarah, for your love, but most of all your patience. Each time you entered my 4am eudaimonia machine to tell me that I needed to snap out of it and help get the kids ready for school, you tolerated my stubborn nature and distain for breaking my hard-to-find focus. You reinforced in me that family comes first and everything else will follow. To look back and think that I somehow completed this work during which was probably the toughest season of our lives together, I really can't make any sense of it other than you were there for me. My work and life are dedicated to you and our children, and I love you very much.

Bibliography

Chapter 1 The Intrepid Consultant

[1] Lurhman, Baz, and Mary Schmich. *Everybody's Free (to Wear Sunscreen)*. EMI Capitol, 1997.
[2] "Teach in Rural, Regional and Remote WA." *Department of Education*, www.education.wa.edu.au/rural-regional-and-remote#:~:text=Our%20Remote%20Teaching%20Service%20is. Accessed 7 June 2024.

Chapter 2: The Legendary Detective

[1] Renwick, David. *Jonathan Creek*, BBC (1998)
[2] Harford, Tim. *DATA DETECTIVE: Ten Easy Rules to Make Sense of Statistics*. S.L., Riverhead Books, 2022.
[3] Reagan, Ronald (1987)
[4] Tarantino, Q. (Director, Writer). *Inglourious Basterds*. Universal Pictures, The Weinstein Company, A Band Apart (2009)
[5] Oakley, Barbara A. *A Mind for Numbers How to Excel at Math and Science (Even If You Flunked Algebra)*. New York, Tarcher, 2014.

Chapter 3: The Master Storyteller

[1] Campbell, Joseph. *The Hero with a Thousand Faces*. 1949. Mumbai, India, Yogi Impressions, May 2017.
[2] Vogler, Christopher. *The Writer's Journey: Mythic Structure for Storytellers and Screenwriters*. London, Pan Books, 2007.
[3] Hollis, Malcolm, and Charles Gibson. *Surveying Buildings*. Hyperion Books, 1991.

Chapter 4: Concrete

[1] *AS 3600:2018 Concrete Structures*. Standards Australia, 19 June 2018.

[2] Hoffman, Mark, et al. *Opal Tower Investigation: Final Report*. Department of Planning and Environment (NSW), 22 Feb. 2019.

[3] Gorrey, Megan. "ACRA | Opal Towers Court Update." *ACRA*, 20 Oct. 2020, acrassoc.com.au/news/opal-towers-court-update/. Accessed 9 June 2024.

[4] "Cross River Rail Embraces Fantastic Plastic Solution." *Cross River Rail*, crossriverrail.qld.gov.au/news/cross-river-rail-embraces-fantastic-plastic-solution/. Accessed 8 June 2024.

[5] Hedges, David, and Eric Spinrad. "When to Take a Seat, When to Make a Stand: The History of 1031-1041 Canal Street, Past and Present." *Nola Tour Guy*, 22 Oct. 2019, www.nolatourguy.com/1031canal/. Accessed 9 June 2024.

[6] Hammer, David. "'300% Overstressed' Beams under 16th Floor Caused Hard Rock Collapse, Engineer Says." *Wwltv.com*, 21 Oct. 2021, www.wwltv.com/article/news/investigations/david-hammer/300-overstressed-beams-under-16th-floor-caused-hard-rock-collapse-engineer-says/289-beb109c6-9df6-43e5-bc7b-24952d99da42. Accessed 9 June 2024.

[7] Razek, Raja. "Grand Jury Decides No Criminal Charges Will Be Filed in the 2019 New Orleans Hard Rock Hotel Construction Collapse That Killed 3 Workers." *CNN*, 6 Oct. 2023, edition.cnn.com/2023/10/05/us/hard-rock-hotel-collapse-new-orleans-no-charges/index.html. Accessed 9 June 2024.

[8] "David Stone Sets up Company to Commercialise Ferrock™ with the Support of Tech 7Launch Arizona." *World Cement*, 20 Nov. 2014, www.worldcement.com/the-americas/20112014/arizona-iron-shell-to-commercialise-ferrock-890/. Accessed 9 June 2024.

[9] Kazmer, Rick. "Researcher Accidentally Discovers Material That's Stronger and Cheaper than Concrete — and Its Potential Is Dizzying." *Yahoo Tech*, 29 Jan. 2024, www.yahoo.com/tech/researcher-accidentally-discovers-material-stronger-120000930.html?guccounter=1. Accessed 8 June 2024.

Chapter 5: Masonry

[1] Charles N, Stoddart. *DETERMINATION of SHERIFF C.N. STODDART in the CIRCUMSTANCES of the DEATH of CHRISTINE JANE FOSTER V.* 25 Feb. 2002, www.scotcourts.gov.uk/search-judgments/judgment?id=083d87a6-8980-69d2-b500-ff0000d74aa7. Accessed 9 June 2024.
[2] *Working Group on Maintenance of Tenement Scheme Property Final Recommendations Report.* Royal Institution of Chartered Surveyors, 2019.
[3] Capon, Joanna. "Decorative Plasterwork in New South Wales." *Australasian Historical Archaeology*, vol. 11, 1993, pp. 43–50, asha.org.au/pdf/australasian_historical_archaeology/11_04_Capon.pdf. Accessed May 30AD.
[4] Lech, Michael. "George Taylor's Improved Fibrous Plaster." *Museums of History NSW*, 15 Oct. 2020, mhnsw.au/stories/general/george-taylors-improved-fibrous-plaster/. Accessed 29 May 2024.
[5] Britain., Great. *Anthrax.* Health and Safety Executive, 1997.
[6] "Boy Hurt after Ceiling Collapses on Pre-Primary Class." *ABC News*, 25 Feb. 2015, www.abc.net.au/news/2015-02-26/boy-hurt-after-ceiling-collapses-on-pre-primary-class-perth/6261848. Accessed 29 May 2024.
[7] "Education Maintenance Stimulus Package." *Www.wa.gov.au*, 30 July 2020, www.wa.gov.au/organisation/department-of-finance/education-maintenance-stimulus-package. Accessed 29 May 2024.
[8] Curry, Andrew. "Gobekli Tepe: The World's First Temple?" *Smithsonian Magazine*, Smithsonian, Nov. 2008, www.smithsonianmag.com/history/gobekli-tepe-the-worlds-first-temple-83613665/. Accessed 11 June 2024.
[9] Rialp, Chad. "Bahay na bato Architecture: 300 Years in the Making." *BluPrint*, 25 Mar. 2024, bluprint-onemega.com/modern-bahay-na-bato-architecture-300-years-in-the-making/. Accessed 11 June 2024.

Chapter 6: Timber

[1] Follett, Ken. *Notre-Dame*. Pan Macmillan, 29 Oct. 2019.
[2] Central, Wood. "French Oak Beams Raise Hopes for Notre-Dame Rebuild." Wood Central, 31 May 2023, woodcentral.com.au/french-oak-beams-raise-hopes-for-notre-dame-rebuild/. Accessed 13 June 2024.
[3] Barthélemy, Jérôme. "A Predictable Surprise: How the Notre-Dame Fire Could Have Been Avoided." *Knowledge.essec.edu*, 16 May 2023, knowledge.essec.edu/en/leadership/a-predictable-surprise-notre-dame-fire.html#:~:text=The%20Paris%20public%20prosecutor. Accessed 12 June 2024.
[4] "Global Forest Resources Assessment 2020 Report Austria." Food and Agriculture Organization of the United Nations, 2020.
[5] "KLH." *KLH Massivholz GmbH*, www.klh.at/. Accessed 12 June 2024.
[6] Waugh Thistleton Architects. "Stadthaus | Waugh Thistleton Architects." *Archello*, archello.com/project/stadthaus. Accessed 13 June 2024.
[7] Barker, Nat. "Fire Safety Expert "Extremely Concerned" about Mass-Timber Buildings." *Dezeen*, 22 Mar. 2023, www.dezeen.com/2023/03/22/fire-safety-concern-mass-timber-buildings/. Accessed 13 June 2024.
[8] "Traditional Japanese Woodwork Techniques." *Excellent Japanese Wood*, excellent-japanese-wood.com/en/technology/column06/. Accessed 13 June 2024.
[9] Nuwer, Rachel. "This Japanese Shrine Has Been Torn down and Rebuilt Every 20 Years for the Past Millennium." *Smithsonian*, Smithsonian.com, 4 Oct. 2013, www.smithsonianmag.com/smart-news/this-japanese-shrine-has-been-torn-down-and-rebuilt-every-20-years-for-the-past-millennium-575558/. Accessed 13 June 2024.
[10] Historic England. "What Is a Conservation Area? | Historic England." *Historicengland.org.uk*,

historicengland.org.uk/listing/what-is-designation/local/conservation-areas/. Accessed 13 June 2024.

[11] Evans, Ian, and National Trust. *The Queensland House : History and Conservation*. Flannel Flower Press, 2000.

Chapter 7: Movement

[1] "Not Us Says Aland, as Mascot Towers Crack Concerns Investigated in 2011." *Urban.com.au*, 7 Dec. 2020, www.urban.com.au/news/not-us-says-aland-as-mascot-towers-crack-concerns-investigated-in-2011. Accessed 13 June 2024.

[2] Stephens, Jodie. "Mascot Towers: Twist in Case of Cracking Apartment Block." *7NEWS*, 27 June 2019, 7news.com.au/news/sydney/mascot-towers-investigation-continues-c-187563. Accessed 13 June 2024.

[3] "Investigation Report - Mascot Towers Development." McCullough Robertson Lawyers, 21 Mar. 2023.

[4] Henriques-Gomes, Luke. "Mascot Towers Residents in Limbo as Berejiklian Promises Action." *The Guardian*, 16 June 2019, www.theguardian.com/australia-news/2019/jun/16/mascot-tower-residents-in-limbo-as-berejiklian-promises-action. Accessed 13 June 2024.

[5] "Legislative Assembly Hansard – 18 June 2019." *Nsw.gov.au*, Parliament of New South Wales, 2019, www.parliament.nsw.gov.au/Hansard/Pages/HansardResult.aspx#/docid/HANSARD-1323879322-105975/link/97. Accessed 13 June 2024.

[6] June 2019, Leith van OnselenThursday 27. "Developers Blame Each Other for Cracking Slum Towers." *MacroBusiness*, 27 June 2019, www.macrobusiness.com.au/2019/06/developers-blame-cracking-slum-towers/. Accessed 13 June 2024.

[7] Santoreneos, Anastasia. "Mascot Towers Is Most "Poorly Built" Building Ever Seen." *Yahoo Finance*, 21 Aug. 2019, au.finance.yahoo.com/news/mascot-towers-is-most-poorly-built-building-ever-seen-004041672.html. Accessed 13 June 2024.

[8] *Australian Lutheran World Service Strategic Plan 2021 to 2026*. Australian Lutheran World Service, 2021.
[9] "Papua New Guinea." *Smartraveller.gov.au*, 2024, www.smartraveller.gov.au/destinations/pacific/papua-new-guinea#:~:text=can%20escalate%20quickly.-. Accessed 13 June 2024.
[10] *BY-LAW No. 514-2008 City of Toronto Municipal Code Chapter 363, Building Construction and Demolition, with Respect to Regulation of Vibrations from Construction Activity*. 27 May 2008, www.toronto.ca/legdocs/bylaws/2008/law0514.pdf. Accessed 13 June 2024.
[11] Australia, Geoscience. "Earthquake." *Geoscience Australia*, 7 Sept. 2022, www.ga.gov.au/education/natural-hazards/earthquake. Accessed 13 June 2024.
[12] "Earthquakes@GA." *Earthquakes.ga.gov.au*, earthquakes.ga.gov.au/event/ga2023kkwzpi.
[13] Ministry for Culture and Heritage. "Christchurch Earthquake Kills 185 | NZHistory, New Zealand History Online." *Govt.nz*, 2011, nzhistory.govt.nz/page/christchurch-earthquake-kills-185. Accessed 13 June 2024.
[14] *The Building Act 2004 (New Zealand)*. 2004.
[15] Holland, Malcolm. *Practical Guide to Diagnosing Structural Movement in Buildings*. Chichester, West Sussex ; Ames, Iowa, Wiley-Blackwell, 2012.
[16] "Foundation Maintenance and Footing Performance: A Homeowner's Guide." *CSIRO*, CSIRO Publishing, 2003.

Chapter 8: Water

[1] Paul Hernandez. "Background." *NIST*, 2 Mar. 2022, www.nist.gov/disaster-failure-studies/champlain-towers-south-collapse-ncst-investigation/background.
[2] "Recertification." *Www.miamidade.gov*, www.miamidade.gov/global/economy/building/recertification.page. Accessed 1 July 2024.
[3] Rodriguez, Rene. "Building Collapse: What to Know about Champlain Towers | Miami Herald." *Web.archive.org*, 26

June 2021, web.archive.org/web/20210626002918/www.miamiherald.com/news/local/community/miami-dade/article252325063.html. Accessed 1 July 2024.
[4] Swaine, Jon. "Engineer Warned of "Major Structural Damage" Years before Florida Condo Building Collapsed." *Washington Post*, 26 June 2021, www.washingtonpost.com/national/champlain-towers-south-surfside/2021/06/26/a509519a-d5de-11eb-a53a-3b5450fdca7a_story.html.
[5] Wodnicki, Jean. "Letter to Residents." 9 Apr. 2021.
[6] "NIST Provides Update on Investigation into the Collapse of Champlain Towers South." *NIST*, 7 Sept. 2023, www.nist.gov/news-events/news/2023/09/nist-provides-update-investigation-collapse-champlain-towers-south. Accessed 1 July 2024.
[7] Wdowinski, Shimon, et al. "Land Subsidence Contribution to Coastal Flooding Hazard in Southeast Florida." *Proceedings of the International Association of Hydrological Sciences*, vol. 382, 22 Apr. 2020, pp. 207–211, https://doi.org/10.5194/piahs-382-207-2020. Accessed 30 July 2021.
[8] Tyson, M. [@MikeTyson]. (2011, May 3). X. https://x.com/MikeTyson/status/65252600425099264?lang=en
[9] "Aligning the Domestic Garden Bore Sprinkler Roster with the Scheme Water Roster Consultation Summary Report." Government of Western Australia.
[10] Royal Institution of Chartered Surveyors. "Review of Entry and Assessment for RICS Membership Summary of Recommendations." June 2024.

Chapter 9: Deleterious Materials

[1] "World Trade Center Health Registry - 9/11 Health." *Www.nyc.gov*, www.nyc.gov/site/911health/about/wtc-health-registry.page. Accessed 1 July 2024.
[2] The Grenfell Inquiry. "Grenfell Tower Inquiry Financial Report to 31 March 2023." The Grenfell Inquiry.

[3] "Update from the Inquiry | Grenfell Tower Inquiry." *Www.grenfelltowerinquiry.org.uk*, www.grenfelltowerinquiry.org.uk/news/update-inquiry-3. Accessed 1 July 2024.

[4] Torero, José. *Expert Evidence - Professor Torero*. 20 Nov. 2018, www.grenfelltowerinquiry.org.uk/hearings/expert-evidence-professor-torero. Accessed 1 July 2024.

[5] Grenfell Tower Inquiry. "Grenfell Tower Inquiry: Phase 1 Report." Oct. 2019.

[6] *The 9/11 Commission Report*. 21 Aug. 2004.

[7] Bisby, Luke. *Expert Evidence - Professor Luke Bisby*. 20 Nov. 2018, https://www.grenfelltowerinquiry.org.uk/hearings/expert-witness-presentations-1 Accessed 1 July 2024.

[8] Conner, Rachel. *Orpington firefighter top ranked woman in London Fire Brigade*. News Shopper. 16 February 2012, https://www.newsshopper.co.uk/news/9536512.orpington-fighfighter-top-ranked-woman-in-london-fire-brigade/

[9] Inquiry Transcript, 27 September 2018, https://www.grenfelltowerinquiry.org.uk/hearings/further-lfb-evidence-29

[10] Voss, Chris. *Never Split the Difference: Negotiating As If Your Life Depended On It*. HarperBusiness, 17 May 2016

[11] Inquiry Transcript, 27 September 2018, https://www.grenfelltowerinquiry.org.uk/hearings/expert-evidence-dr-glover

[12] Inquiry Transcript, 19 June 2018, https://www.grenfelltowerinquiry.org.uk/hearings/expert-witness-presentations-0

[13] Apps, Peter. *Show Me The Bodies: How We Let Grenfell Happen*. HarperBusiness, 10 November 2022

[14] "Hebel." *CSR Dwelling*, dwelling.csr.com.au/. Accessed 1 July 2024.

[15] Davis, Anthony. "Building Fire-Resistance with 3D Printed Concrete Homes in Los Angeles." *Highways Today*, 3 Jan. 2024, highways.today/2024/01/03/3d-printed-concrete-homes/. Accessed 1 July 2024.

[16] Molitch-Hou, Michael. "Dubai Seeks to 3D Print 25 Percent of Its Buildings by 2030." *Engineering.com*, 6 May 2016, www.engineering.com/dubai-seeks-to-3d-print-25-percent-of-its-buildings-by-2030/. Accessed 1 July 2024.

[17] "WAM." *Wam.ae*, 2024, wam.ae/en/article/b1qrfjf-trakhees-issues-first-licence-for-building. Accessed 1 July 2024.

[18] Johanson, Simon. "Dexus Snaps up Waterfront Place Tower, Eagle Street Pier Retail Site for $635m." *The Sydney Morning Herald*, 22 June 2015, www.smh.com.au/business/companies/dexus-snaps-up-waterfront-place-tower-eagle-street-pier-retail-site-for-635m-20150622-ghu40b.html. Accessed 1 July 2024.

[19] Ford, Trevor. *Spontaneous Fracture of Glass due to Nickel Sulphide Inclusions - Risk Management and Development of a Non Destructive Testing System*.

[20] "Flawed Beauty: The Problem with Toughened Glass - IELTS Reading Practice Test." *Mini-Ielts.com*, mini-ielts.com/222/view-solution/reading/flawed-beauty-the-problem-with-toughened-glass. Accessed 1 July 2024.

Chapter 10: Building Services, Code Compliance, and Contaminated Land

[1] Bernstein, Nina. "Bellevue Hospital Evacuates Patients after Backup Power Fails (Published 2012)." *The New York Times*, 1 Nov. 2012, www.nytimes.com/2012/11/01/nyregion/bellevue-hospital-evacuates-patients-after-backup-power-fails.html?_r=0. Accessed 1 July 2024.

[2] *Celebrating 10 Years of the Ability Suite*. Manchester United Disabled Supporters Association , 2013, mudsa.org.uk/wp-content/uploads/2014/02/abilitysuite10.pdf. Accessed 1 July 2024.

[3] Environmental Protection Agency. *Community Information, Contaminated Land and Groundwater at 227-231 Barkly Street, Brunswick*. Jan. 2004, webarchive.nla.gov.au/awa/20050602011512/pandora.nla.gov.au/pan/50296/20050601-0000/937.pdf. Accessed 2 July 2024.

[4] Australian Government Defence. *PFAS Investigation and Management Program Snapshot*. Feb. 2024, www.defence.gov.au/about/locations-property/pfas. Accessed 2 July 2024.

[5] Ombudsman Victorian . "Brookland Greens Estate - Investigation into Methane Gas Leaks." Oct. 2009.

[6] Ritchie, Mike. "Why Aren't Landfills Listed as Contaminated Sites?" *Inside Waste*, 9 May 2024, www.insidewaste.com.au/why-arent-landfills-listed-at-contaminated-sites/. Accessed 1 July 2024.

[7] Australian Government Department of Prime Minister and Cabinet. *Best Practice Regulation Guidance Note Value of Statistical Life*. Oct. 2021.

Chapter 11: Environment, Social & Governance

[1] Cromwell Property Group. "Cromwell Settles $166 Million Tuggeranong Office Park." *Market Index*, 30 June 2008, www.marketindex.com.au/asx/cmw/announcements/cromwell-settles-166-million-tuggeranong-office-park-XX200721. Accessed 3 July 2024.

[2] Australian National Construction Review. *State-of-The-Art Office Building Welcomes Thousands of Government Workers*. 2016.

[3] The Weekly Source. "Cromwell Property Group Revealed as 50-50 Partner in New LDK Healthcare Village and Aged Care Development in Canberra." *The Weekly SOURCE*, 28 Aug. 2018, www.theweeklysource.com.au/topic-aged-care/cromwell-property-group-revealed-as-50-50-partner-in-new-ldk-healthcare-village-and-aged-care-development-in-canberra. Accessed 3 July 2024.

[4] Government of South Australia Department for Trade and Investment. *Planning and Design Code*. 18 Jan. 2024, plan.sa.gov.au/__data/assets/pdf_file/0004/1335028/South-Australian-Planning-and-Design-Code-Version-2024-1-18-January-2024.pdf. Accessed 3 July 2024.

[5] Riahi, K., Rao, S., Krey, V. et al. *RCP 8.5—A scenario of comparatively high greenhouse gas emissions*. Climatic

Change 109, 33 (2011). https://doi.org/10.1007/s10584-011-0149-y
[6] Thomson, A.M., Calvin, K.V., Smith, S.J. et al. *RCP4.5: a pathway for stabilization of radiative forcing by 2100.* Climatic Change 109, 77 (2011). https://doi.org/10.1007/s10584-011-0151-4
[7] Zhang, Yating, et al. "Projections of Corrosion and Deterioration of Infrastructure in United States Coasts under a Changing Climate." *Resilient Cities and Structures*, vol. 1, no. 1, Mar. 2022, pp. 98–109, https://doi.org/10.1016/j.rcns.2022.04.004.
[8] Financial Stability Board. "About the FSB." *Fsb.org*, 2019, www.fsb.org/about/. Accessed 3 July 2024.
[9] TCFD. "Task Force on Climate-Related Financial Disclosures." *TCFD*, 2022, www.fsb-tcfd.org/about/. Accessed 3 July 2024.
[10] Task Force on Climate-Related Financial Disclosure. *Recommendations of the Task Force on Climate-Related Financial Disclosure*. June 2017.
[11] Cranston, Matthew. "Midtown Centre to Replace Brisbane's Ageing Government Towers." *Australian Financial Review*, 5 Dec. 2017, www.afr.com/property/midtown-centre-to-replace-brisbanes-ageing-government-towers-20171205-gzz39o. Accessed 3 July 2024.
[12] NSW Government. *Embodied Carbon Measurement for Infrastructure*. Apr. 2024, www.infrastructure.nsw.gov.au/media/ak2o0bqg/decarbonising-infrastructure-delivery-measurement-guidance.pdf. Accessed 3 July 2024.
[13] Lukasik, Tara. "Advanced Window Technologies: The Latest on Thin Glass." *Www.glassmagazine.com*, 21 Sept. 2023, www.glassmagazine.com/article/advanced-window-technologies-latest-thin-glass. Accessed 3 July 2024.
[14] Orr, John, et al. *A Brief Guide to Calculating Embodied Carbon*. July 2020.
[15] IEA, IRENA & UN Climate Change High-Level Champions (2023), *Breakthrough Agenda Report 2023*, IEA, Paris https://www.iea.org/reports/breakthrough-agenda-report-2023, Licence: CC BY 4.0

[16] CarbonCure. "CarbonCure Technologies | from Carbon to Simply Better Concrete." *CarbonCure Technologies Inc.*, www.carboncure.com/. Accessed 3 July 2024.

[17] "About PT Blink." Ptblink.com, 2017, ptblink.com/about/#section=section-2. Accessed 22 Jan. 2025.

Chapter 12: Resilience

[1] Mirvac. "Brisbane's Heritage Lanes First to Achieve Australia's Greenest Certification." *Www.mirvac.com*, 6 Sept. 2023, www.mirvac.com/en/about/news-and-media/brisbanes-heritage-lanes-first-to-achieve-australias-greenest-certification. Accessed 3 July 2024.

[2] Ramos-Ruiz A, Wilkening JV, Field JA, Sierra-Alvarez R. *Leaching of cadmium and tellurium from cadmium telluride (CdTe) thin-film solar panels under simulated landfill conditions.* J Hazard Mater. 2017 Aug 15;336:57-64. doi: 10.1016/j.jhazmat.2017.04.052. Epub 2017 Apr 24. PMID: 28472709; PMCID: PMC5607867.

[3] Kotzen, Benz, et al. *Fire Safety Risks of External Living Walls and Implications for Regulatory Guidance in England.* Vol. 139, 1 May 2023, pp. 103816–103816, https://doi.org/10.1016/j.firesaf.2023.103816.

[4] AboutNL. "How Does the Nederlands Live below Sea Level? - the Netherlands." *AboutNL*, 8 Sept. 2023, aboutnl.com/how-does-the-nederlands-live-below-sea-level/.

[5] "Brisbane Flood Resilient Ferry Terminals." *COX*, www.coxarchitecture.com.au/project/brisbane-flood-resistant-terminals/. Accessed 3 July 2024.

[6] The B1M. "Torre Reforma: Building an Earthquake Proof Skyscraper." *Www.theb1m.com*, 2 Nov. 2016, www.theb1m.com/video/torre-reforma-building-an-earthquake-proof-skyscraper.

Chapter 13: Data & AI

[1] Elara AI, elaraai.com/. Accessed 13 Jan. 2025.
[2] "The Hidden VFX in Live Sports." YouTube, Corridor Digital, youtu.be/qkWWcjeL_zM?si=8VRXmeN3-n0Zi9_2. Accessed 13 Jan. 2025.
[3] "Fireside Chat with Ilya Sutskever and Jensen Huang: AI Today and Vision of the Future | GTC Digital Spring 2023 | NVIDIA On-Demand." NVIDIA, 2023, www.nvidia.com/en-us/on-demand/session/gtcspring23-s52092/?ncid=so-yout-561702. Accessed 14 Nov. 2024.
[4] Gray, Charles M., and David A. McCormick. "Chattering Cells: Superficial Pyramidal Neurons Contributing to the Generation of Synchronous Oscillations in the Visual Cortex." *Science*, vol. 274, no. 5284, 4 Oct. 1996, pp. 109–113, https://doi.org/10.1126/science.274.5284.109. Accessed 11 May 2023.
[5] Real Estate Institute of New South Wales. "REINSW Appoints Australia's First AI Board Advisor." *Reinsw.com.au*, 30 May 2024, www.reinsw.com.au/Web/News/Media_Releases/2024/05-May/ai-board-advisor. Accessed 3 July 2024.

Further Reading

Many practicing building surveyors I know enjoy a small physical collection they keep within arm's reach for their immediate reference. I offer the following list on a basis no more than my personal preference. If you are starting out in this field or looking to add to an existing collection, I hope you find it valuable.

Aurelius, Marcus. *Meditations*. S.L., Collectors Library, 2020.

Bryson, Bill. ***Bryson's Dictionary: For Writers and Editors***. London, Black Swan, 2016.

Chudley, Roy, et al. ***Chudley and Greeno's Building Construction Handbook. 12th ed***., Abingdon, Oxon; New York, NY, Routledge, 2020.

Douglas, James. ***Building Surveys and Reports***. John Wiley & Sons, 2010.

Douglas, James, and Bill Ransom. ***Understanding Building Failures***. Routledge, 2007.

Edmund George Warland. ***Modern Practical Masonry***. Routledge, 2015.

Evans, Ian, and National Trust. ***The Queensland House: History and Conservation***. Mullumbimby, QLD., Flannel Flower Press, 2000.

Griffith, Saul. ***The Big Switch: Australia's Electric Future***. Collingwood, Vic, Black Inc, 2022.

Hackett, Mark, et al. ***The Aqua Group Guide to Procurement, Tendering and Contract Administration***. Chichester, West Sussex, Wiley Blackwell, 2016.

Hetreed, Jonathan, et al. *Architect's Pocket Book*. Routledge, 2017.

Holland, Malcolm. *Practical Guide to Diagnosing Structural Movement in Buildings*. John Wiley & Sons, 2012.

Hollis, Malcolm, and Charles Gibson. *Surveying Buildings*. Coventry RICS Books, 2010.

Hollis, Malcolm, and Royal Institution of Chartered Surveyors. *Pocket Surveying Buildings*. Coventry, RICS Books, 2007.

Macdonald, Susan. *Concrete Building Pathology*. John Wiley & Sons, 2008.

Matthys Levy, et al. *Why Buildings Fall down: How Structures Fail*. New York, W.W. Norton, 2002.

McDonald, Roxanna. *Illustrated Building Pocket Book*. Routledge, 2016.

Neville, Adam M, and J J Brooks. *Concrete Technology*. Prentice Hall, 2010.

Oldenburg, Ray. *The Great Good Place: Cafés, Coffee Shops, Bookstores, Bars, Hair Salons, and Other Hangouts at the Heart of a Community*. Philadelphia, Da Capo Press, 1999.

Pallasmaa, Juhani. *The Eyes of the Skin*. Chichester Wiley, 2012.

Prentice, Andrew, et al. *Newnes Building Services Pocket Book*. Routledge, 2012.

Seeley, Ivor H. *Building Maintenance*. Bloomsbury Publishing, 1987.

Seeley, Ivor H. *Building Surveys, Reports and Dilapidations*. Basingstoke, Macmillan, 1991.

Watt, David. **Building Pathology: Principles and Practice**. Oxford; Malden, Ma, Blackwell Pub, 2007.

William Hyslop Irvine. *Surveying for Construction*. London; New York, Mcgraw-Hill Book Company, 1995.

Yao, Mariya, et al. *Applied Artificial Intelligence: A Handbook for Business Leaders*. Middletown, De, Topbots, 2018.

Index of Buildings

Accessory Dwelling Unit, California, USA	131
Address Downtown, Dubai, UAE	116
ALWS Hospitals, Madang, Papua New Guinea	77
Bosco Verticale, Milan, Italy	183
Brookland Greens Estate, Cranbourne, Australia	152
Centenary House / 19 National Circuit, Barton, Australia	165
Champlain Towers South, Florida, USA	85
Cross River Rail, Brisbane, Australia	41
Floating Pavilion, Rotterdam, Netherlands	184
Grenfell Tower, London, England	114
Hard Rock Hotel, New Orleans, USA	42
Heritage Lanes, Brisbane, Australia	174
Hōryū-ji Temple, Ikaruga, Japan	64
Ise Grand Shrine, Ise, Japan	64
Kellerberrin District High School, Kellerberrin, Australia	175
Lacrosse Apartments, Melbourne, Australia	113
Lakanal House, London, England	113
Mascot Towers, Mascot, Australia	71
Meckering Primary School, Meckering, Australia	82
Midtown Centre, Brisbane, Australia	164
Moai, Rapa Nui, Easter Island	54
Notre-Dame de Paris, Paris, France	57
Old Trafford, Manchester, England	147
One Eagle, Brisbane, Australia (formally Waterfront Place), Brisbane, Australia	132
Opal Tower, Sydney, Australia	35, 73
Parliament House, Barton, Australia	165
Pyne Gould, Christchurch, New Zealand	83
Queenslander Houses, Queensland, Australia	65
Rosemead Preparatory School, Dunwich, England	129
Shepherd's Court, London, England	115

Singlewell Primary School, Gravesend, England	129
Soward Way, Tuggeranong, Australia	160
Stadthaus, London, England	61
Stonehenge, Salisbury, England	29, 54
Taipei 101, Taipei, Taiwan	74
Torre Reforma, Mexico City, Mexico	185
Tuggeranong Office Park, Tuggeranong, Australia	160
Waterfront Brisbane, Brisbane, Australia	134
World Trade Centre, New York City, USA	87, 112
Accessory Dwelling Unit, California, USA	131
Address Downtown, Dubai, UAE	116
ALWS Hospitals, Madang, Papua New Guinea	77

List of Abbreviations

ACM	Asbestos Containing Material
ACP	Aluminium Composite Panel
ADA	Americans with Disabilities Act
ADU	Accessory Dwelling Unit
ALWS	Australian Lutheran World Service
AI	Artificial Intelligence
AIBS	Australian Institute of Building Surveyors
AMP	Asbestos Management Plan
API	Application Programming Interface
AS3600	Australian Standard for Concrete Structures
ASHI	American Society of Home Inspectors
ASR	Alkali-Silica Reaction
AUD	Australian Dollar
B2B	Business-to-Business
BBA	British Board of Agrément
BCA	Building Code of Australia
BIM	Building Information Modelling
BMS	Building Management System
BRE	British Research Establishment
BREEAM	Building Research Establishment Environmental Assessment Method
BS	British Standards
BS8414	British Standard for fire performance of external cladding systems
BS8484	Lone working solutions standard introduced by the British Standards Institution

BSI	British Standards Institution
BTEX	Benzene, Toluene, Ethylbenzene, Xylene
CAD	Computer-Aided Design
CAHPI	Canadian Association of Home & Property Inspectors
CSIRO	Commonwealth Scientific and Industrial Research Organisation
CLT	Cross Laminated Timber
CNC	Computer Numerical Control
CO_2	Carbon Dioxide
CPU	Central Processing Unit
CTO	Chief Technology Officer
CTS	Community Title Strata
CV	Curriculum Vitae
DCTH	Deductions, Correlations, Theories, Hypotheses
DDA	Disability Discrimination Act 1992
DEI	Diversity, Equity, and Inclusion
DJAG	Department of Justice and Attorney General
DtS	Deemed to Satisfy
EAF	Electric Arc Furnace
EPA	Environmental Protection Authority
ESG	Environment, Social & Governance
FR30	Fire Door with a Fire Resistance Rating of 30 Minutes
FR60	Fire Door with a Fire Resistance Rating of 60 Minutes
FSF	Financial Stability Forum
FSG	Fire Survival Guidance
GHG	Greenhouse Gas

GLT	Glue Laminated Timber
GPT	Generative Pre-trained Transformer
HKIS	Hong Kong Institute of Surveyors
HOA	Homeowners Association
Hz	Hertz
IEA	International Energy Agency
ISO	International Organization for Standardization
ITE	Inspección Técnica de Edificios (Technical Building Inspection, mandatory in Spain)
JAHI	Japan Association of Home Inspectors
KC	King's Counsel
KPMG	Klynveld Peat Marwick Goerdeler (professional services firm)
LEED	Leadership in Energy and Environmental Design
LFB	London Fire Brigade
MBIE	Ministry of Business, Innovation, and Employment (New Zealand)
MP	Member of Parliament
MRICS/FRICS	Member/Fellow of the Royal Institution of Chartered Surveyors
NABERS	National Australian Built Environment Rating System
NAHI	National Association of Home Inspectors
NAO	National Audit Office
NCC	National Construction Code (Australia)
NIST	National Institute of Standards and Technology (USA)
NSW	New South Wales
NZS	New Zealand Standard

OAM	Order of Australia Medal
OC	Occupation Certificate
ODEC	Observation, Deduction, Elimination, Conclusion
PCB	Polychlorinated Biphenyls
PCE	Perchloroethylene (also known as tetrachloroethene or PERC)
PFAS	Per- and Poly-fluoroalkyl Substances
PWD	Persons with Disability
RAAC	Reinforced Aerated Autoclave Concrete
RBS	Royal Bank of Scotland
RCP	Representative Concentration Pathway
REINSW	Real Estate Institute of New South Wales
RFI	Request for Information
RICS	Royal Institution of Chartered Surveyors
SAHITA	South African Home Inspection Training Academy
TCFD	Taskforce for Climate-Related Financial Disclosures
TDD	Technical Due Diligence
UPS	Uninterruptible Power Supply
USD	United States Dollar
UST	Underground Storage Tank
UX	User Experience
VIC	Victoria
VT	Volcanic-Tectonic

ABOUT THE AUTHOR

Craig JL MacDonald is a Chartered Building Surveyor and fellow of the Royal Institution of Chartered Surveyors. He has been active in property and construction for over 20 years. Holding an honours degree in Building Surveying from Heriot-Watt University, Edinburgh, MacDonald is known by his peers for bridging traditional building pathology thinking to modern technology themes. He has researched and contributed various articles to RICS Built Environment Journal. He co-founded Beyond Condition – a platform which streamlines custom data entry for building inspectors – with his business partner and computer scientist, Ben Ihle. MacDonald is currently practising as a building consultant based in Brisbane, Australia, applying his expertise in commercial property technical due diligence to the Australian and New Zealand property market.

www.ingramcontent.com/pod-product-compliance
Lightning Source LLC
Chambersburg PA
CBHW051536020426
42333CB00016B/1954